HOPE you will ENjOy
reading SOME of these
Adventures of so long
Ago. Especially:
NEW GUINEA
South Pacific
W W II

Best personal regards

George Wamsle

American Fly-boy

American Fly-boy

George Wamsley

VANTAGE PRESS
New York

Published by Vantage Press, Inc.
516 West 34th Street, New York, New York 10001

Manufactured in the United States of America
ISBN: 0-533-10341-X

Library of Congress Catalog Card No.: 92-90824

0 9 8 7 6 5 4 3 2 1

Some is for real
Some is as remembered
Some is as told by others
Some is imagination
Some is fantasy
Some is scary
Some is unbelievable
Some is exciting
Some is boring

But:
All was, and is, interesting to me

Contents

Foreword   ix
Introduction   xi

1. Mostly Earlyhood   1
2. Family Life: Grace E., G.W., Charlo   7
3. Growing Up   21
4. Orchestra and Airplanes   30
5. Military Flight Training   40
6. Flight over the Pacific   64
7. Guadalcanal   79
8. New Guinea   98
9. Back in the United States   181

Foreword

"I was always a lucky kid." That was my husband George's frequent response to the question as to why so many things and events in his life have been extraordinarily good and turned out extraordinarily well. Yet there is something more to be said. Anyone born in the United States in 1915 starts out as "a lucky kid." The fact that it happened in the glorious state of Montana was an added happy circumstance.

At any rate, over the years I've known George and his family there has grown in my mind a question: what makes the difference between what would seem to be an ordinary life and something much greater than that? George would never agree that his has been extraordinary through any action or purpose on his part, but he would, I think, agree that he has been the recipient of great blessings. His "only living sister" (the only one he ever had) and I have "hounded" (his words) him to write about some of these blessings just for the sake of his family and for some close friends. Most important among the latter group would be his extended family: "the squadron."

BARBARA WILSON WAMSLEY

Introduction

Perhaps the reason for writing about various events in my life is to attempt to answer a question posed over the years since World War II by many people. I refer to those who wonder just what was in the makeup of young Americans who would respond, as so many did, to the call to service. We came from all walks of life, too young to be specialists, but eager to use up our energy and to show our adaptability.

We did know something about American history and our traditions, from Revolutionary days of defending liberty. Whether we knew it or not, liberty made us the way we were.

Trying to think back forty-five to sixty years in order to recall events during World War II and before isn't easy. There are doubts about the accuracy of some of those recollections, but to me they have become absolutely accurate as written here. Take into consideration that it is easier to recall the good luck of finding a dime in the dust than to remember the bad luck of some stern schoolmarm hitting you on the hand with a ruler for no reason at all. The good memories make those "olden years" into "Golden Years." Also, a certain confidence was gained by having been in the top ten in my high school graduating class. There were only six in that class.

I always liked airplanes. The day Dick Johnson landed his grand 1930s Stinson Travelaire cabin airplane in a neighbor's pasture while he was on a local barnstorming trip was a big day for me. For one dollar I was permitted to actually feel the controls of a machine in flight, going through the air on its own power. A wish fulfilled. A thrill that had been anticipated for some time.

The actual opportunity to participate in aviation came while I was attending the University of Montana. A federal program called Civilian Pilot Training (CPT) was offered as part of the curriculum, and for credit yet! I was at the head of the line to sign up. My easy time in military flight training was a result of the preliminary CPT program at Johnson's Airport in Missoula.

When the military decided to make me a C-47 troop carrier pilot instead of my first or second choice, fighter pilot or heavy-bomber pilot, that was still all right. The assignment turned out to be perfect for me.

In the early stages (circa 1942) of the land-air war in the Pacific, rigid rules and procedures were nonexistent. As an example: If any written orders were ever "cut" sending me from the United States to New Guinea, I have yet to see them. We were just thirteen crews with thirteen airplanes that were needed in that great big Southwest and South Pacific area. Surely someone would tell us what to do. Sometimes someone did.

We were pioneers in WW II, as were so many others. And our 33rd Troop Carrier Squadron did its part.

As we were island-hopping across the Pacific, en route to New Guinea, the U.S. Marines were attempting to dislodge the Japanese from their southernmost advance at Guadalcanal. Not that the marines would ever admit they needed help, nor would the U.S. Navy admit that a lot of their ships were sunk at Iron Bottom Bay, but someone saw a chance to assist those forces with a few C-47 troop carrier planes. Bull Halsey himself, the supreme commander of that area, intercepted some of us and told us to haul some much needed supplies right into Henderson Field on Guadalcanal. That November of 1942, with our unarmed and unescorted planes, we did as he directed. The marines prevailed and the Japanese never advanced any farther southward in their quest for new territory.

Onward we went to New Guinea, where the Japanese controlled nearly all of the continent except Port Moresby. They were about thirty miles from the port, working their way through the jungle, hoping to deny that new general in Australia (Douglas MacArthur) a foothold in this primitive country. One day and about 1,000 miles after sneaking away from Bull Halsey, we set up our tents in Port Moresby.

For two years, although it seemed like ten, the 33rd lived and died as loyal, patriotic American citizens defending the interests of the United States as our assignment dictated.

Perhaps my relating some of the events dating from my childhood to "maturity" will be of interest to you.

American Fly-boy

Chapter 1
Mostly Earlyhood

How do you start at the beginning? Whether I'm writing or talking, I notice it always gets back to "me" or "I," and I don't care for that. Maybe a little conceit or vanity is okay, but I sure don't want other people to think about me that way. It is embarrassing to write about one's self. On the other hand, if a lot of interesting experiences and some that are quite unusual just happen to a guy, perhaps there isn't anything too bad about reliving them by the written word.

One of my favorite remarks has always been: "I was a lucky kid." I was born in Manhattan, Montana, on Easter Sunday morning, 1915. Thank you, Grace and G. W. Wamsley, for being my parents; that was one of my first lucky breaks. However, I had been around quite awhile before I was really convinced I wasn't a girl, because I'd heard my mother tell her lady friends for years that George Junior was supposed to have been a girl, since she already had two boys. The ladies would look at me and giggle, shake their heads, and then get back to their card games.

The Indian reservation in a very small town where Dad had built and owned a general merchandise store was an unusual place to grow up. Not many people lived in Charlo, Montana. We didn't have an adequate number of kids to put together a ball game or to play "kick the can" without using all the kids in town. Sometimes when playing baseball we had to use a dog or two as our outfielders. Sometimes we even used girls, if they were tomboys, as well as the dogs to make up a playable game.

We kids made up our own fun and games. Without paved streets or good sidewalks, we couldn't use trikes or bikes. The small rocks in paths and roadways were major hazards. Besides, a trip across the whole town was only a brisk five-minute walk. Watching the Northern Pacific freight trains switch a few cars from the grain elevators or the stockyards was exciting, as well as a learning experience in safety. Climbing around amongst the piles of lumber at Erwin's Lumber Yard or building hiding places out of egg crates from Dad's storage shed and a few cream cans from the cream station gave us many hours of challenging games. I'm not sure that kind of happy childhood would sell in today's market, but ours sure beat the scourge of modern times: television.

All of the trash from the store basement, such as packing boxes, gunnysacks, stale bread, and old merchandise, would routinely be brought to a bonfire area in back of the store by one of us workers for burning. There were no pollution regulations to comply with, so a variety of items were disposed of in this manner. On this particular day we had just gotten a brisk fire going and were sitting around it when suddenly there was an explosion. The explosion seemed like a major event to us, but it was probably minor. My face got smacked in about a hundred places (maybe it was only six or eight, but it seemed like a hundred) by unknown rockets shot from the fire. We got to the house in seconds, hollering all the way. My saintly mother finally got us all to quiet down enough so she could administer Unguentine to the black spots on my face and scrape the chunks of black goo off our clothes. When she determined no one was seriously injured we were sent on our way. Certain we had found a bomb left over from World War I, we were a bit cautious making our way back to the fire. As we carried a bucket of water and a few sticks to stir up the ashes back toward the bonfire, we became convinced that someone had planted dynamite. After we doused the fire, we learned that our attacker had been a two-pound can of blackberries that had been thrown away because the berries were fermenting inside the can.

Dad, G.W., treated us very well: that's Joe, Jim, George, Pink, Fran, Marney, and Gene. Dad made us all take our turns helping in the store when we became old enough to run a broom, stock the shelves, and do other dirty work he obviously didn't want to do himself. As time marched, each one of us became qualified so we each got to (read that: *had to*) open the store promptly at 7:00 A.M., spread the sweeping compound, sweep the aisles, and start filling the shelves in case any items had been sold the previous day. Some days that part, filling shelves, was an easy job. Depression times. Whatever that was.

Our dog, Chum, was a very important part of that 7:00 A.M. opening ritual. With Chum it was a big wag of the tail, which shook his entire hind end in obvious excitement. He would let out a small bark of welcome and lick the hand that he knew was about to give him his morning treat. Chum always got two or three chocolate-covered mints. We placed them along the top rail of the fence so he could jump up and snare them with his long tongue. Happy dog. Happy kid.

Animals were an important part of our entertainment. Chum, like so many dogs, exhibited very basic allegiance if he got adequate attention and "found": that's room and board in western talk. I presume Chum gave equal devotion to whomsoever came along on the way to adventure or who might offer a chocolate in response to a sincere look or a vigorous wag of the tail. Chum was always available if a pickup game of baseball was about to be played; if it looked like the truck was going for water from the well, because he could dominate all the dogs along the way with wild barks of defiance; if wild horses got into the yard and needed to be sent away; if true fellowship and companionship were about to be needed by some kid; or if someone came out with a gun and would obviously need a retrieving dog to fetch any game successfully shot. Chum would just plain laze around inside or outside the house waiting for action of any sort by anyone who was a true friend.

3

On one of the rare occasions when one of the kids needed to be disciplined for a minor oversight or even a major indiscretion, Dad had the best solution I've ever heard of. He'd grab a horsewhip off the rack and hustle Chum down into the store basement, shouting threats loud enough for all of the neighborhood to hear that he was about to whip the dog to within an inch of his life. Then Dad would pop the whip and shout some more so he could be heard a half-mile away. All of the kids, whether family, neighbors, or just a passerby, would be promising to "never do that again" or agreeing to "pile the wood right now" or "go home to help get supper." Dad would always extract some promises from the wrongdoer before he could quit punishing the dog. Of course we would agree to everything Dad wanted. Then they would come out of the basement, Dad with the whip over his shoulder and Chum dancing up and down and licking the hand of his tormentor. Sure enough, Chum would have chocolate-covered saliva running down his chin.

But even a good dog doesn't live forever. As Chum grew older some more mature mortals could be heard mumbling, "Ole Chum isn't going to be with us much longer," or "How old is Chum now?" or "What will happen when Chum is gone?" Dad kept his eye on Chum and occasionally decided the dog was too sick to live. One day Dad put a gun in the car and put Chum in the backseat. We knew what to expect but couldn't talk about it because it would mean losing a member of the family. Dad didn't come back for a long time. Interested parties just had to hang around, but there wasn't much joy. There was plenty of gloom and sadness. Finally, after too long a time, the car reappeared; turns out he drove clear up to McDonald Lake, which was about twelve miles away. We were all anxious to find out how it went. Dad stopped the car, reached over the backseat, and opened the door. Chum staggered out and made a look like, "We sure had a nice long ride." Dad just said, "He seemed to be a lot better right after we left the house." Dad was not tough. Chum went to the back porch and curled up on his blanket for a good sleep.

4

Dogs weren't the only pets the kids had in Charlo. Pink got a cow that he was instructed to milk at the proper time. Also, he had to shovel the other product out into the pasture. I doubt if he ever did. Shovel it out there, I mean. And he never did learn to drink milk.

Jim and Marney each got horses to call their own. I often wondered why. My major experience riding a horse, and a miserable one it was, was on a high school sneak day. A number of us saddled some borrowed horses, packed a lunch, and headed off on a grand ride to the National Bison Range at Moiese. That's a long way even to drive a car, let alone amateur cowboys riding that far just for fun. When we got to the range headquarters, we saw some buffalo up close, ate our sandwiches, did our toilet, and followed the command of some long forgotten trail boss to "mount up." We mounted, it started to rain, and we headed the many miles back home. For most of us, our backsides were killing us already. Our legs, hands, and shoulders were raw, stiff, or sore or all three. We approached the long ride home with about as much enthusiasm as the Charlo football team playing Missoula. *None*. Each mile we rode was more wet and cold than the previous one, and miserable. Whoever the fool was who thought up this day of torture should have been horsewhipped.

By the time we finally arrived on Charlo's main street we were the riding dead. I was too mature to cry and hurt too much to walk. Besides, there were some other schoolkids waving us home. By that time, my cayuse had his head down between his front legs, his eyes were closed, his legs were trembling, and I know he wanted to die also. Just as I did. Either he tripped over a toothpick or he just plain gave up. Anyway, he stumbled and his forefeet collapsed and his rider (me) flew ass-over-teakettle across the saddle horn, over the horse's neck and head, and into the mud in the street. I didn't think I would ever get up. When I finally struggled halfway to my feet, I got the worst humiliation of all. My pants were torn down the front. Quite a tear, too. I was tired to death, cold, wet, embarrassed, angry, and sore all over, and to top it off, some rotten kids laughed at me. I think I said, "I don't care if I never see any of you again. And I know darn well I'll never get on another horse!" Must have meant it; never been on a horse since.

Chapter 2
Family Life: Grace E., G.W., Charlo

Grace E.

Mother was often referred to as Grace E. The *E* is for Elizabeth. Grace's mother died shortly after my mother's birth. Various relatives reared her in a good Catholic atmosphere. She ultimately became an accomplished hatmaker for the Hennessy Department Store in Butte. I think that is where she hooked onto G.W., but that may not be accurate. They didn't know at the time they met that they would raise seven kids, all boys except Marney.

After three fast ones, Joe, Jim, and George, was probably when Grace and G.W. decided it would be a good time to borrow some money and build a general merchandise store, so that the staples would be available in some degree for a large family. They chose Charlo, Montana. Most of the family were, and still are, very grateful for that decision. I can't exactly say why, but it was a great family life for many years. A small town is just better than the larger ones for kids.

Grace insisted on a large house, and she got her way. Our house was large for that place at that time and quickly became a hub of activity for babies, kids, and the ladies and gentlemen of the area. The only water was from a cistern that was filled frequently by water hauled in cream cans from a town pump down by the coulee just north of town. The water in the cistern was brought into the house by a hand pump in the kitchen. Years later, a city water tank and underground lines provided adequate water for household use, and that ended the life of the hand pump in the kitchen. The outdoor toilet was near the coal shed and garage. Sometime during that era the gas lamps and coal oil lanterns were replaced by a direct-current Kohler electric generator, owned by the Pete Sorenson Power Company. Eventually Mother got an indoor bathroom, too.

Seems to me it should have been a very easy life for Grace with all those helpers coming along and all those modern amenities, but I know it was not. She allocated many chores to various members of her "staff." Sometimes they got done. Other times, when the staff was busy playing games, shooting baskets, doing school homework, or involved with other miscellaneous worldly pursuits, the household chore schedule would be temporarily forgotten. On second thought, I don't recall school homework interfering with the chores. But somehow Grace would manage alone and supper would be ready and ample and enjoyed by family, friends, and various drop-ins. Sometimes store customers would find the store locked and just drop by to see if somebody would open up. If those drop-ins timed it right, they could sit down for a bite of dinner or a piece of cake at least, until one of us young assistant managers could go unlock the store for whatever the customer needed. Imagine, Grace did that for forty or fifty years. With all the dinners Grace served to drop-ins, the store could have prospered much more if she had been a cash customer.

That big old house, which doesn't seem so large anymore, was a stopping place for a wide assortment of folks. Included among the visitors were neighbors, both kids and adults, college classmates, and friends from out of town. Also, politicians (Democrat) and even an occasional traveling salesman frequently stopped by. The doors were never locked. A goodly number of people knew that they were special friends, so they would usually just walk in. They always knew who was home anyway. In summer, the large fenced yard with grass and flowers and trees hosted many an impromptu picnic or "cook in, eat out."

Most of the time there were extra people over for dinner. One of those individuals was a guy from Missoula, a friend of my brother Pink, I think. Buck was an only child of adoring parents who knew he could do no wrong and approved of everything he chose to do. When he thought he might like to stay on at our house for a while, no request was made, no permission given, no notice taken. Buck stayed so long he graduated from Charlo High School. He was a popular guy around town: played football, mowed the lawn occasionally, and helped some of the local girls with their studies. I presume he even had a key to the store. When he broke his leg, another penalty of growing up, Mother nursed him without hesitation and provided plenty of TLC. I think she just embraced him as one of her own.

Grace was a very pious person. She couldn't, or wouldn't, do anything wrong or think disparagingly about anyone. She did, however, smack an errant child occasionally, but perhaps that was justified. Grace saw to it that all those in the house who should do so went to church on Sundays. And she never missed an opportunity to serve the Lord.

For example, I remember one time when the State of Montana Fish and Game Commission decided that the fall pheasant season would not open till Sunday at noon. That decision was against tradition and without logic. How would the people from Cutbank, Great Falls, and Butte return home from the field at a reasonable hour after becoming tired and hungry from the rigors of chasing those wily birds? Furthermore, it would pose a problem for those hunters who had chosen to commit revelry on Saturday night and then had nothing to do until noon on Sunday.

That's where this story about Mother and her dedication to church comes in. Quite a few citizens had checked in at our house on Saturday, and many others began arriving quite early on Sunday morning. At about nine-thirty, Mother announced, "There are quite a few here that should be going to Mass this morning. Mass at D'Aste is at ten o'clock. So let's get going so we won't be late."

She would have gone to church had she been the only one. So what the heck? Going to church would humor Grace, and it would fill in some of the time waiting for noon opening of pheasant season. Several cars set out on the five- or six-mile journey to the little church at D'Aste, and the hunters arrived with great good fellowship to disperse among the faithful of the small group of ex-miners from Butte whose ancestry included Irish, Polish, and German nationalities.

In this story about Mother, another hero becomes a part of the incident. Augie was an interesting character who got around a lot in Charlo and nearby towns and was a retired businessman. The story is that Augie had been a competent contractor who had been very successful and retired at an early age. Augie had a cabin on the lake and kept active with his boats, cars, travels, and visits to our home. On this particular day, Augie had been relaxing at our house for several days, drinking beer, casing the countryside, and spreading good cheer at every friendly tavern.

To complete the story: The priest arrived at church on time, chose a couple of altar boys, and got into his vestments. With a big smile at the congregation, the priest addressed the Holy Altar. Gladys, who sometimes played the old organ, did not appear. Mother saw her opportunity to serve. She tapped Augie on the shoulder and asked him if he would play a few songs of glory and praise. To the congregation's surprise, he could and he did.

Augie sang. Mother and Dad sang. The people sang. The priest sang. The small building shook. At Consecration and Communion time all became most reverent, holy, quiet, and prayerful. What a change in the spiritual attitude of the hunters from the morning scene at our house. The priest gave all a heartfelt blessing, thanked the congregation, kissed the altar, and began the recessional. Augie and the organ and the people and the priest broke into a rousing recessional that would have rocked St. Patrick's Cathedral.

What a hero Augie was, Mother also. Her friends gathered around and asked over and over, "Where did you find such a

10

talented singer and organist?"; "Who is he?"; and "Will he be living here?" When we got back to the house, Augie fell asleep on the davenport and the gang went hunting. Mother looked over him. She'd wake him up occasionally, give him some soup and sometimes tomato juice, and smile on him and whisper almost to herself, "My, what a dear boy!"

Hunting was important in our neck of the woods. Most everyone who lived in western Montana from Eureka to Darby or attended college in either of the two state institutes of learning was aware that Charlo was the prime game bird–hunting area of the state. Chinese ring-necked pheasants were in plentiful supply, with good cover in the irrigation ditches. The fall season of the year was usually most pleasant, and roads along almost all one-mile section lines made it possible for the less hardy or fit to walk across a field and pick up a ride, even if covered with cattails or down and wearing muddy boots.

Dignitaries of the state's larger corporations, bankers, and garbage collectors all seemed comfortable getting out of their uniforms and donning dress and hardware to head for the hunting fields around Charlo. A large percentage of them would arrive at Wamsley's the night before or early on the morning of opening of pheasant season. There was no guest list. Everyone seemed to be welcome. Our saintly mother would have lots of coffee ready long before daylight, so those that ventured into the house could grab a cup of hot coffee, a glass of juice, a bottle of beer, and bullets (shells) if needed and hurry off to their various rendezvous points.

Excitement filled the air in anticipation of the grand sport. A conglomeration of dogs would be so excited they'd quiver and dance around their masters, licking hands. The dogs would walk through any available mud and hop into the cars as the doors opened. Some minor foul-ups would always occur, so a few hunters would be late arriving at their agreed meeting place. This group would miss the opening barrage as daylight appeared. That was the big moment, rather like the opening of the curtains on a major opera by the most famous troupe in the most popular opera house. Those that were late or those that forgot their shotguns or couldn't find their shells or gloves and held up their friends from this opening salvo would sure catch it from the others. Funny how a couple of hours later, after walking six or eight miles and shooting a box or so of shells, a goodly number would head back toward the house, lugging their birds, to rest up so they could start all over again. And of course Mother would have a large kettle of chili ready to be consumed. There would also be available plenty of beer, bourbon, pop, and milk and an atmosphere for relaxing, resting, bragging, good-natured kidding, and joviality. About noonish, somehow she would place platters of freshly fried chink (pheasant) out for general consumption.

I never wondered in the past, but I sure have ever since, Who helped her? One thing that made it easy for her was the nearby availability of the chink supply. It was just outside the kitchen door on the back porch. People would throw their birds there till they covered the floor. Then any early departee or those too tired to continue could take as many birds as they chose back home to show as trophies to the folks they had left there.

On one of these occasions, a gorgeous collegian from Missoula came to the valley. Intelligent, of good family, charming and sophisticated and a good dancer, she was also athletic enough to walk over hill and coulee and dale, shotgun in hand, for a few hours. All went well until there came a call of nature. No one responded to her discreet inquiries as to how to handle the situation until some gentleman assured her it was proper and okay to rest near a haystack. She probably did. As I understand it, girls can't take a leak very well while standing up. So upon attempting to do it some other way, an extra strain was put on the zipper of her new Levis and it jumped the track.

Obviously, she could not go around holding her gear up all day. Someone suggested she go into town and have Mrs. Wamsley fix it. Grace could do anything. Once our huntress found the proper house, it was only minutes before the problem was solved. However, in the meantime, the warmth and serenity of the house outweighed the requirement of rejoining the hunt with its dogs, mud, bird killing, and the shouting and fun of the chase. A bowl of chili, a glass of milk, and the companionship of Grace and G.W. made for an instant and forever lasting friendship. Those who got to know Barbara's parents had a mutual experience. The saga of the zipper is still recounted around many a camp fire these many years later. Again, talking about the comforts of home, I am reminded that Mother would always call on someone to say the grace before eating at suppertime. They should. It was a beautiful spread. Lots of meat, potatoes, bread, vegetables, and nearly always a big bowl of gravy. I repeat: Grace got her groceries wholesale.

Sometimes one of the younger kids would be insubordinate at suppertime and would be dispatched to the clothes closet, where he could yell and make promises to his heart's content behind the closed door. I guess those bad kids were learning the power of rank as well as a little discipline. I'm not aware of any prisoners in the closet who ever did any damage while there, but I did hear of one person, a girl, who when so confined did spit on her parents' clothes.

At the end of supper, the management would repair to the living room to visit or to listen to good music on the old Edison thick record phonograph. 'Twas not always tranquil, though. One incident, which was not typical, involved the three cleanup crew members who were clearing, washing, and drying the supper dishes. They had sort of a conveyor system in action. Number one got the dishes to the sink, number two did the washing and drying, and number three did the putting away. In order to save some steps, and being of high spirits, number one picked up a bowl containing two leftover baked potatoes. He hollered at number two, who was ten or fifteen feet away, "Hey, catch!" and tossed the bowl and potatoes to him. Number two was very agile and quick besides. He reached out both hands and caught the two baked potatoes, one in each hand. The crash of Mother's best china bowl was loud and scary. That was one time Grace E. lost her cool.

Quite a few things often went wrong about that time of day. On one occasion when G.W. was not in the house, the staff and their friends were acting up so loudly they couldn't hear Grace admonish them to quiet down. She got up, put on her coat, and walked out the door into a very dark night. Our town had no sidewalks and minimal streets, and our neighbors were scattered. When Mother didn't return in what some of us considered a reasonable length of time, we headed out to see what disaster might have befallen her. Visions of a sprained ankle or our mother stuck in an irrigation ditch or even fending off hungry coyotes went through some heads. Finally someone spotted her and hollered to her, "Oh, there you are!"

"Yes," she said. "I just stepped outside for a breath of air." She got a lot of fresh air in that length of time, but she never mentioned the incident again.

G.W.

You would have to call Dad a slight disciplinarian, because he didn't make a big deal of setting out rules and regulations for our daily duties and responsibilities. But somehow we knew who was the boss. He quietly got things he wanted done, and generally they were done his way. One incident comes to mind that proved his way was usually best. He instructed us subordinates to use a chunk of wood or a piece of an old tire to absorb the shock when unloading a barrel of vinegar off the Northern Pacific Transport truck. "Put the barrel on its side. Roll it to the tailgate, and use your leg as a lever as you roll the barrel out. Then twist it enough so that the rim of the barrel will hit the preplaced bumper at about a forty-five-degree angle. Pull on the top and use the momentum to set the barrel in an upright position."

14

The advice sounded easy. Unloading the barrel was not hard to do and did not take a lot of strength. Besides, the method had worked successfully for a bunch of years, so I don't know why one guy (no names please) decided to change the system. He ignored the part about the shock absorbers and just rolled the barrel off the tailgate smack on the floor of the store. *Smack* was the right word. I can tell you for sure that fifty gallons of vinegar coming out of a totally smashed container all at one time is a hell-of-a-mess. Vinegar ran to the right under the bags of flour and into the egg crates. It flowed to the left amongst the garden tools, the brooms, and the nuts and bolts. But most of it went straight ahead to the floor-level grill and down on the hot coal-burning furnace in the basement. It created one tremendous unpleasant smell. I don't recall details of what happened next, nor do I know if the word *cool* was in general usage at that time, but I think on that day Dad did lose his cool and took some kind of remedial action.

Perhaps Dad had more good days than bad. He put things in perspective. Not to worry if one of the kids wrecked the car or blew up the store. It was always a blessing if no one was hurt. If the cash sales were under ten dollars for the day Dad would always say the charge sales looked okay. Of course, lots of those charge accounts were never paid, so it really wasn't okay. Dad seemed to be in total control of the bookkeeping for the store. After all, accounting was just adding income items together and then subtracting outgo items. This made a number that we thought of as probably a hefty profit. Dad had been a bookkeeper for Beckwith's at St. Ignatius and at other mercantile establishments in Belgrade and Manhattan, Montana. The way his assistant managers knew that the times were not all easy for him was if they saw a cloud of cigarette smoke bloom over his office corner, followed by the pushing aside of his ledgers and journals. They knew the next step would be for Dad to put on his hat and stomp out the back door covered with gloom. Later when he returned, Dad would make some slight admonition that we had

to hold back on spending. This would be mentioned sort of apologetically.

Holding back on spending wasn't too hard for Dad's assistants to handle. To help him out, we would just not tally in the sales book everything that went out for clothes, groceries, and sundries for the house account. We could easily see that to cut that house expense in half we must write down only half those items that should have been written down, and expenses were reduced accordingly. I don't think Dad would have thought this a proper way to run the business.

Jim used this same logic and had a good deal going. He would bake a three-layer chocolate cake and frost it with thick chocolate frosting. He sold it to the bachelor who ran the grain elevator, for seventy-five cents. Of course Jim had used ingredients from the store, but since he didn't charge them to the house account, it looked like clear profit to him. It also cut down on recorded expenses.

Dad, G.W., did have some fun. He would ice-skate on cold Sunday afternoons if there was a group willing to join him. The sport ended when he had a major collision with another skater and wound up with the point of someone else's skate in the bridge of his nose. It sure did bleed, but he didn't let it happen a second time. He gave up skating.

Sliding off snow-covered roads during the winter and getting stuck in the mud during rainy season were expected where we lived. Dad always had a pretty good, large car, both dependable and capable of hauling numerous people. The first one I really remember was a Case. The car must have had a powerful engine, because if extreme care wasn't used in backing it out of the garage, the gears in the differential would be stripped and the car would be out of commission until Harley Bran could order repair parts from the factory back east.

Harley was sort of an "on-call" mechanic. The time Dad was going to take a bunch of kids to the circus in Missoula, he asked Harley to come along. On the way, every so often, Harley would get out on the running board and get a close listen to the engine as

we cruised along the road at about twenty-seven miles per hour. After a good, thorough listen, he would holler, "Seems to be doing just fine, George!" Then Harley would make his way back to his assigned seat. Maybe an efficient way, but not a safe way to inspect the mechanical progress.

Charlo

As I remember, that store was just like a community center. People liked to visit there amongst the dry goods and even buy merchandise sometimes. They all had charge accounts. Some of them paid their accounts. Many did not. The importance of the store can be established by noting the plaques given to G. W. Wamsley Company from such important manufacturers as Goodyear Tire and Rubber Company, McCormick-Deering Harvester Company, Socony Vacuum Oil Company, Standard Oil Company of New York, Del Monte, Pacific Fruit Company, and Eddy's Bakery.

Although the store was located on the Flathead Indian reservation, not many Indians patronized us. The Indians were located principally in the communities of St. Ignatius, Dixon, Ronan, and Pablo. The full-bloods were exceptionally good people. Their word was their bond, and they were ashamed of the few whose actions reflected adversely on the tribe. Occasionally one of the Flatheads would come by the store and want groceries on credit until the next government check would come. G.W. could communicate with them, something he had picked up while working at St. Ignatius Mission. They often insisted upon leaving some item of beaded ceremonial clothing as security for the groceries they needed. The items were stored in the vault until their owners came back at the promised time, paid their bill, and recovered their security. Some of the items left were really beautiful beaded pieces of art. As far as I know, none were ever forfeited.

The family store on the Indian reservation (that _is_ a horse!)

All the family liked to take Sunday drives. G.W. would explore new roads, forest trails, mountain passes, scenic spots, lakes, and streams. When he couldn't find a new adventure, he'd repeat an old one. One of the longer but better trips was through Missoula, up past Salmon Lake, past Seeley Lake, past Swan Lake, to Bigfork and then down the beautiful and scenic west shore of Flathead Lake and back home. Quite a trip. On one particular day, as we passed somewhere along Seeley Lake, Dad made this observation: "There is a Forest Service road that takes off somewhere about here and cuts through the Mission Mountains. We can get right up over the mountains and go down the other side. We'll go by Upper Jocko and Lower Jocko lakes. Then the Jocko River has to run down to lower ground and through Arlee and Ravalli. Won't be too far from home then."

Mother, being overly conservative, said, "George, we only have a picnic lunch for the six of us. Those roads may not be too good and if we get stuck, who knows when we would be found?"

"Aw, this car will go anywhere," Dad replied.

And it did. We didn't get stuck. But after we left Lower Jocko Lake, the road was only a dikelike pile of clay dirt running beside the river. Its width was exactly the same as between the center of one front tire to the center of the other front tire, so it seemed there was half of one tire hanging over the river and half of the other hanging over thin air. I'm sure you know what happened then. It started to rain. The only thing more slippery than wet clay is 3-in-1 oil, and that particular road got mighty wet and slippery. It was dangerous.

We passengers became unruly until finally, upon Mother's demand, Dad let us all out to walk and slide along behind the car. Dad must have been expendable. He knew he was in for it so deep he might just as well slide into the river. If he was lucky, we would just lose the car and we could all walk home in a day or two. Mother told us all to pray, and we did, with gusto. The car didn't fall in the river, and the rain finally stopped. I guess that's when we really understood the power of prayer. I was afraid God didn't work up in those mountain canyons, but He was watching out for somebody. Probably Mother.

Speaking of slippery, the family was invited up to the Hockers' home for Thanksgiving dinner. They lived on a beautiful site at the foot of the Mission Mountains, straight east of Ronan. Everyone dressed up in his best clothes. One of the kids had his first suit with pants on. Dad fueled the old Buick, and a carload headed out. As was often the case in those days, the road was wet and slippery. On the incline toward the Hockers', the Goodyear Double Eagle tires, one of the many brand names sold at the store, just couldn't keep the heavy car going forward. Almost, though. So Dad made everyone except Mother get out and push. And it helped some. The Buick needed just another few feet to get to level ground, so the kids pushed and shoved from the back with their last ounces of strength.

The kid with the new suit didn't want to be a laggard, so he put forth a superhuman effort. Somehow his footing was not too good. Both feet went the wrong direction at the same time just as the extra pushing paid off. The Buick went over the hump, and the kid fell flat on his face and chest and waist and knees and shoes and elbows in the muddiest part of the road.

Mother was only halfway through her Rosary when we arrived at the Hockers' door. The killer instinct usually dissipates faster than you can say the Rosary. That is, if the potential killer exercises this option.

I've prattled on here much too long about things remembered. But a lot of those happenings long ago surely must have been the basis of what made most of our family feel that we lived a good life. There is an obvious point to be made: You didn't have to become a captain of industry, the richest person around, or a Nobel prize winner, but there wasn't any reason you couldn't do it, either. Living through a depression without even knowing there was one might just build some character. Growing up in Charlo, Montana, at that time with my family in the house behind the store, amongst those people with their varied characteristics and personalities, was a priceless gift. We didn't have to grow old to appreciate it. We always did appreciate it.

Chapter 3
Growing Up

Our friend Augie, the church organ player, was quite a joker. He was often at his best during pheasant-hunting season. One day as he and all the other good and loyal hunters grew more and more tired, as well as more and more full of lemonade or other thirst quenchers, our hero suddenly got into one of his play-acting characters. This time Augie decided it might be interesting to play the part of a game warden. So he tried it. He put his hand up and stopped a car loaded with hunters on their way out of the area. He very politely asked how their hunt had been. They said they had "filled up," meaning they had gotten their limit of birds.

"That's great," said Augie. "Were they good big roosters?"

"Oh, yah," they responded, offering him a little touch out of their bottle. They passed a few words about the good hunting, nice weather, and sportsmanship. Very congenial group.

Then Augie indicated it would be good for him to inspect the birds for health and size and just generally do his duty. So he had the hunters open the trunk.

"My God! You are six birds over the limit. How come?"

Their response was to share another sip of that lemonade, or whatever.

Then Augie said, "I must have miscounted. You are only two birds over, so I'll have to take away two."

The hunters were pleased and satisfied that their lemonade had helped in the solution to a potential problem, and they drove away. Augie played game warden again. Within an hour, he claimed he had fourteen birds. He didn't want to work at it any longer because he was afraid he might get half-drunk from that lemonade!

One evening during duck-hunting season, Jim was in charge of the store and I was assisting; Grandpa Wamsley was across the street at the scales weighing in a load of baled hay. The folks had gone to the big city on a buying trip and had not yet returned home. Someone came into the store, I think it was Chuck Krichendal, and said he wanted to buy a shotgun. The total stock of guns was one shotgun and one .22 caliber repeater rifle. Jim got down the shotgun and talked to Chuck about the merits of the gun. They handed it back and forth a few times, took imaginary aim at a duck or two, and tested it for balance, and both decided it was a good Remington shotgun.

They'd been leaning over the counter that had corduroy pants and a pile or two of work shirts stacked on it. I was across the counter, being a smart aleck, practically looking down the barrel, just being a general nuisance, until Jim told me to beat it. It appeared I wasn't welcome, so I backed off a few steps and left them to entertain themselves.

Ker-boom-swish! It could only be a shotgun blast from an "unloaded" gun. All hell broke loose. I headed toward the back door, Grandpa came charging in the front, Jim and Chuck probably both wet their pants. The store smelled like burning cordite. There was a hole in the wall about twelve inches across. It was up near the ceiling, just over the glass dry-goods and sundries display counter. A sheet of cardboard covered that reminder for a good number of years. My brother Fran could probably tell for just how long.

Times weren't always easy in Charlo for businesses or banks. The little bank at Charlo closed. No idea how much was in the store account there, but as to how much the store could not afford to lose, it was very close to 100 percent. Several of the kids had amounts ranging from six dollars to as high as twenty-six dollars in their own bank accounts, so the bank closing was a major financial setback for us all. The store account was then established at St. Ignatius. Some time after the failure of the Bank of Charlo, Dad got a call from the financial man at the Missoula Mercantile Company. Missoula Mercantile Company was our benefactor and principal source of credit and merchandise. The man told Dad there was a good chance the Bank of St. Ignatius would not open tomorrow morning or ever again. Unfortunately, G.W. had just mailed, that afternoon, one of the largest deposits he had ever made, probably around six or seven hundred dollars. That was almost a life-and-death amount. It was the future of the store or the unfuture of the store.

Dad called the bank manager and told him that he would be in St. Ignatius in the morning to pick him up at his house and that together they would go to the St. Ignatius post office as soon as it opened to retrieve that piece of mail. What else he told him I don't know, but Dad returned to Charlo with his deposit intact. Disaster was averted.

This is a story about Indians; communication with them was not always easy for non-Indians. In the early 1930s, the Montana Power Company entered into a deal with the Flatheads and the Kootenai to build a sizable dam across the Flathead River just below Flathead Lake. This dam would be used to generate electricity, help control the level of the lake, and give the Indians a nice income almost forever for having leased the land to the power company for the generating plant. The Indians had acquired the land by treaty with the U.S. government, but they had never received training about making deals. They signed, by making their mark, an "X" on a bunch of documents.

When the grand dam structure was completed, it was appropriate to have dedication ceremonies. The Indians were properly represented by two great chiefs, Chief Charlo and Chief Koostahtah. They were each about eighty years old and about five feet tall. They came to the dedication dressed to the hilt in elaborate traditional formal Indian attire, including eagle feather headdresses.

Beautiful. Two senators represented the U.S. government. Representatives of the Montana Power Company included Frank Kerr, president, after whom the project was named; John C. Ryan, vice president; and C. H. Tornquist, construction superintendent of a New York general contractor. The Indian dignitaries were Meschel, Coeur D'Alene chief; Martin Charlo, Flathead chief; Koostahtah, Salish chief; and Baptiste Messiah, also a chief. Other important participants were A. J. Brower, a prominent state senator, and Roy Ayers, governor of Montana.

I was there, not as a VIP, but because our high school jazz band had the only public address system around and I set that up (with Don Burbank's help) so that the crowd could be entertained and could hear the speeches. Duncan McDonald may have been the interpreter. We were in a picturesque setting. Green lawns surrounded the nice homes that had been built just next to the river for managers of the dam. The guests enjoyed lots of ice cream, pop, and many buffalo sandwiches. The buffalo sandwiches may have been supplied by the Indian Ladies Aid Society.

For that time, in that setting, in that country, it was truly awesome. The dam towered above our heads. It was probably one of the largest man-made structures most of the participants had ever seen, excepting the guys from Washington. To look up toward the top of the dam from way down there made everyone realize this was not just another ribbon cutting. It was a piece of history being made right here.

Each of the Washington dignitaries made his remarks and gave his praises to the chiefs for their farsightedness and their cooperation. Each phrase had to be translated by Duncan so the Indians would know what had been said. The power company people, governor, and other visiting potentates all had their say and talked about the great future the Indians could look forward to, thanks to this solid economic project.

Perhaps the honorable chiefs didn't understand what was meant by "future." They were happy, well fed, full of pop, and excited when their time finally came to be introduced and to make some remarks about what a great day this was. I don't remember which chief got up first, but one did and his speech into that mysterious microphone, as translated by Duncan, went like this: "The Indians are happy to be here. The Indians are happy the white people are here. The Indians are happy that this dam will provide our tribes with more money than we ever dreamed."

The Indians ate the rest of the buffalo sandwiches, drank the remaining pop, and then just headed for home to take off their hot ceremonial garments. Don and I took down the speaker system and went home also. It was a no-pay job for us, too.

Speaking of buffalo sandwiches reminds me that my brother Joe and his lovely wife, Margaret, somehow acquired ownership of the small country store at Moiese. The store was actually within the boundary of the National Bison Range. The headquarters of the Bison Range was about a half-mile from the store. Since a good relationship existed twixt the store people and the two families it took to run the entire park, everyone connected with the store got all the buffalo meat they could use. It's not as good as beef, so say I, but it's not bad either. As a matter of interest, that park produced and raised to maturity a real albino buffalo. All white except for some black hair between his horns and his light blue eyes. He was very sacred in the lore of the Indians. His picture was on a lot of postcards.

The store consisted of the merchandise area, a small enclosed corner area containing the U.S. Government Post Office, a grain elevator, two gas pumps, and a two-bedroom living area. Population of the town was two, Joe and Margaret, until their son, Rod, was born.

Joe liked to drive into Missoula, about forty miles away, and did it every chance he got. If one of his customers needed something not available that day at the store, Joe would turn over the management to Margaret and head off to Missoula. He would locate what he had been sent for, get some groceries at the wholesale house, stop by the Elks Club, and then head back to Moiese. Joe did a lot of good things for a lot of people. On the Fourth of July, Joe would always acquire a bunch of fireworks and go to Charlo to shoot them off in front of a big crowd. That was great, and generous, too.

Joe seemed to have the answer to most problems and would take the necessary action to resolve them. He even hired me a few summers to help out down there while he and Margaret gallivanted off to more exciting areas. Of course for me to take charge I had to become an official assistant U.S. postmaster. Probably my first big appointment.

Joe did a couple of things that were not what the average person would do. Like the time when a bunch of skunks got under the store. It didn't phase him. He'd taken ROTC at Bozeman and knew about guns, so he just got out a gun and shot the skunks. There were three, I think, and he killed them dead. The store had to be closed for over a week. That wasn't such a bright idea, to shoot those skunks.

Joe, as postmaster, became quite a stamp collector. He put together an excellent collection of used and unused stamps. People came from miles around to examine Joe's exhibit and to buy and trade to expand their own collections. Joe heard about some monks over in Spokane who had large numbers of used stamps that they would sell. He went there and bought their entire supply. That was twelve 100-pound gunnysacks filled to the brim with stamps! After working on that treasure for over a year, Joe had only gone through one sack. So he packed them all up and took them back to Spokane and donated them back to the same monks. Although that deal didn't work out too well, Joe's stamp collection still exists to this day.

At the upper high school and the lower college age, about seventeen or eighteen, is about the time many people begin to exercise their intellect. So for me things changed around Charlo when I reached that time of life, about 1932. There was more to life than fun and games. It dawned on me that people must decide what

G.W. with Chum and nephew, Rod, 1932

to do with the rest of their lives, and there were a lot of decisions to be made.

The other kids and I made a small clubhouse out of an old unused building, and that became the "think tank" of the settlement. Membership was not very strict. We had to permit some guys outside the basic core group to participate especially if they knew a bit about carpentry or glazing or painting. I guess every "man" who lived in the village and was of the proper age group was a member, and most any with the same qualifications but living on the nearby farms were welcome, too. But no girls were allowed. The loose-knit charter group was most likely Pink (for whom I had vouched), Bob (his dad owned the lumberyard and we always needed lumber), Alan (who couldn't work on glass or use a hammer for fear of damaging his piano artist's hands), Don (who was older but was a qualified electrical improviser), and Scotty (an orphan who drifted through and who had taken trumpet lessons, which might come in handy). There must have been others equally qualified, because we had a lot of big-time talent.

We cleaned away the cobwebs, fixed the broken window-panes, nailed on the walls, put an old room heater in, built a bench or two to sit on, and then started contemplating what to do with ourselves in light of current world conditions: the depression years. We didn't smoke or spit, but it seemed that there was a lot of laughing and wondering about "what if . . . ?" All logical subjects would be discussed to some degree. It was some time before any topic would get on the unofficial agenda more than once. Not that we were negative; we just had a lot of ideas to consider.

My contribution seemed to lean toward aviation. I don't mean starting an airline company or a manufacturing plant, just a dream about how great it might be to ride in an aircraft. A big dream would be about becoming a pilot. The thought of controlling all the power needed to make a plane fly through the sky and going from place to place without getting lost and then landing the machine in a designated space without crashing was a Buck Rogers style subject good for a lot of speculation. I'm not sure the other guys were so hot on the topic, but I sure was. To be outdoors and occasionally pick up the distinctive sound of an airplane flying slowly to or from Missoula, over along the Mission Mountains, was a thrill that went from my head to my toes.

There were many things to wonder about concerning the airplane. How can a propeller make a machine fly? How can a pilot make it go left or right, or up or down? Why do some planes have two wings and some only have one? In my memory I get a vivid picture of a two-place, open-cockpit biplane chugging by on this side of the clouds along the Missions. The pilot was obviously going very fast, probably sixty or seventy miles per hour, and I wondered what he was thinking about, how it felt, was he lost? Of course at that time, I didn't realize that he could see the railroad tracks that went all the way to Polson and then he could go lengthwise across Flathead Lake to Kalispell, where there was a landing field. Another particular image at that time must have been in 1927, because I was bouncing a ball off the side of the store and praying—a young man's fond hope and wish is a prayer, isn't it?—that Lindbergh would make it safely across the ocean and land in Europe. He did. Not only did Lindbergh become everybody's hero: he also opened up a new chapter in the potential use of the sky and developed an industry that was to exceed the wildest speculation of that time. I wanted to be part of that industry.

Chapter 4
Orchestra and Airplanes

Orchestra

A major project that spawned from those lofty seminars in the clubhouse was the development of a jazz band, which offered unlimited potential for fun, future, fame, and glory. About that time (say 1931 or 1932), one of the truly universally praised pleasures was provided by the advanced institutions, the big bands. The names and the different styles of such famous bands as the Dorsey Brothers, Paul Whiteman, Guy Lombardo, Benny Goodman, and many others became well known to most all ages and still are fondly remembered fifty years later. We had a unique opportunity because we already had one person who had bowed to his mother's demands to take some piano lessons, and it turned out he liked doing it and had a natural talent. Alan's cutting personality and his good looks would stand us in good stead when we made it to the big time. Bob Erwin was the next best-looking with his curly black hair, so he was assigned lead saxophone in case we ever acquired a sax. As time passed we somehow found enough local youths who were quite interested in becoming accomplished jazz musicians, with enthusiastic visions of becoming suave, popular specialists in this chosen field.

John McNees wanted to play a trumpet, so he got one, and when Scotty came along with his own trumpet, and being already knowledgeable about the sound of the C scale, our brass section was on the way. Later when another band member obtained a valve trombone—valve, not slide—a sound style just like the big guys was possible. One more sax, which Glen Bingham worked to master, would give us the smooth factor that would be important when and if we ever played for the slow dancers. Howard Jaten melded it all together with a bass horn. Except, of course, the need for the important position—drums. I accepted.

Later on, after word leaked out that we were destined for the big time, other sorts of talented people approached us wanting to join in. Another saxophone, a banjo, and a female vocalist gave us the flexibility to play all kinds of dance music. Several of the already anointed practiced enough on an extra instrument so that a bigger reed or brass or string sound could be rendered. The practicing or rehearsing went on for a long, long time, perhaps because we had a lot to learn and we just weren't very fast at learning. But it was always fun. We could use the school gym in the evenings unless some school or other high-priority group function had been promised use of the facility. We'd blow and stomp and start again and again but never seemed to tire of it. After high-level discussions about sounds, speeds, volume, repairs, speculating about our future and other plans and dreams, we'd often move on to G.W.'s store for watermelon, cheese and crackers, or pop and cookies, always with more talk about our fast progress and our lofty goals. No time for mischief here.

Eventually, we were prepared for the big step. We offered to play for a school function in front of a real live audience. (Some hangers-on had been stopping by occasionally just to see what was going on and what the noise was about, but they didn't seem to be very impressed. There was no applause or encouragement. None of them knew how to dance anyway.)

Our first live appearance was from the stage in the gym looking right down on the heads of the local PTA gathered for an official meeting. We were in clean clothes, hair combed and scared to death. But we gave them what they wanted to hear: "Darkness on the Delta," and "Moon over Miami," and one other super tune. The applause was deafening, but we hadn't prepared for an encore, so we just gave them "Darkness on the Delta" one more time.

After a lot of fine-tuning (get it?) our melodies, we ventured out into the competitive world of paid employment up and down the dance halls of western Montana. The crowds got larger and the gigs more frequent as fame spread. Phil Sheridan, from the Davenport Hotel in Spokane, sent us hundreds of professional arrangements of the popular tunes of the day, so our expenses were minimal. We played for charity, for junior proms, at Post Creek, at Pleasure Island in Whitefish, and at many fund-raising events in all the surrounding communities. The pay was not too good, but it was a great experience.

An important extra benefit of the orchestra experience was learning about the big names that are so well known even today. We'd know about most of the artists in each of those bands, what they played, and what the leader was like. If they were playing a date in the West, we knew about it and often got to go see and hear them. The Dorsey Brothers at the Paladium in Los Angeles, Benny Goodman at the Palamar, Eddie Duchin in Helena (Alan played second piano for about an hour), Paul Pendarvis in Missoula, and even Russ Morgan, Wayne King, and of course Phil Sheridan. It was a learning experience that has never been forgotten.

I wonder who sold and kept the proceeds from my instruments? My drums and clarinet!

Airplanes

Airplanes became a fascination early on—not the Wright Brothers, but sometime after that when we started hearing about aircraft that really flew with people in them and carried some mail from one location to another. Names like Billy Mitchell, Doolittle, Rickenbacker, Lindy, Luke, Ryan, and the Red Baron weren't

The orchestra, 1933

exactly household names, but their bravado in flying machines and their confidence in the future of aviation gave a lot of us an inner feeling that their pioneering would lead to a new and exciting period. Powered flight through the air! *Wow!* My first flight was from a dirt field just this side of Ronan, right beside the graveled road. Johnson Flying Service of Missoula had just acquired a new five- or six-passenger cabin Travelaire from the factory in Wichita. Dick Johnson took it around the state as a barnstormer. He'd fly low over the chosen community and then land near town and wait for the curious to come and look. They did. For one cent per pound the five or six passengers could get an exciting ride of about twenty or thirty minutes' duration, over the farms and cities, and then rattle, bump, and stop on the dusty ground from which they had taken off. I had enough cash for a ride and was almost at the head of the line for the first trip. Dick must have seen the gleam in my eye, because he suggested I sit in the seat beside him. That flight was a thrill that never left me and the start of a love affair with flying machines. When we landed, Dick suggested I just keep my seat, so I got two rides for the price of one.

The Johnson Flying Service, owned by Dick and his brother Bob, became prosperous and famous. They pioneered the smoke jumper program for the Forest Service, and to this day the U.S. Forest Service Air Fire Control adjoins the Johnson Airport in Missoula. It's great to be able to call Bob and Dick Johnson friends.

In the late 1930s the U.S. military formulated a plan to give a significant number of aspirants the opportunity to get some rudimentary skills and experience in caring for and flying small aircraft. Arrangements were made between the military and some state universities whereby qualified applicants in the second year of college could elect to take some ground school and flight training for college credit and at minimal cost. Johnson Flying Service was one of the first of these contract schools, and I was one of the first to jump at this chance to actually get some flight training. The flight-training program seemed like it would be a lot more fun than the boring classes I had been taking. Perhaps social studies, Book-keeping I, elementary math, music appreciation, and other solid subjects would ultimately make me a better person, but I wasn't making much progress in them anyway. So my emphasis was put on the CPT program.

Ten of us began the process of learning to start the engine, taxi out, check the instruments and controls and the fuel gauge, and then head down the runway as directed by the flight instructor. When that forty-horsepower engine got the Piper Cub up to about forty miles per hour and it was about to gravitate (leave the ground), real flying began. The instructor would shout a lot of instructions through the gaspord tubes from his mouth to the student's ears. With his steady hand on the stick, he would get the Cub going in the right direction at the right speed and the proper elevation so that everything fell into place. The propeller pulled the plane forward as the wings provided lift to keep it in the air. As long as you had fuel, you could go anywhere.

Learning to fly was so easy it wasn't long before the instructor announced it was "solo time" and each student became master of his machine. After a couple of short cross-country trips of 60 or even 100 miles away from home, a minimum number of hours learning engine repair and maintenance, and absorption of a few safety requirements, the U.S. government issued the students aircraft pilots' licenses. About the first day after I got mine, I got Tom Bird and we took a Cub out for a joyride. We decided as long as we had all this freedom, why not go up in the mountains and look for some good ski slopes? After about an hour of flying around snow-covered peaks and valleys, up creeks and down rivers, we decided we'd found a potentially good spot—and not too far from town either.

After landing and getting out of my parachute, I was beckoned by Dick Johnson. "I've been watching you through the glasses," he said. "Do you think that was an intelligent thing to do, to be flying around those mountains where the snow is deep and the wind uncertain, and you with only a few hours of instruction?"

"Seemed okay to me," was my meek answer.

"Well," he said, "I gotta tell ya. I like it, too." I never did know if that was a reprimand or not.

The second phase of the CPT program was when the fun began. Those who passed Phase I and were otherwise qualified got to apply for Phase II. That meant more intensive ground school classes, some even at night, but most important was the machine in which we would be training: a two-place, open-cockpit Waco biplane with a big, powerful engine. A mean, tough, rotten instructor (which Dick Johnson was not) was our nemesis. He let us know we wouldn't make it through the training period, that we were basically no good as pilot prospects, but we'd probably kill ourselves anyway because we didn't pay enough attention to him, so it didn't really matter. On our first ride with him, he volunteered to demonstrate some things the aircraft could not do, but also some aerobatics that he could easily do because he was the "greatest" (he said) and because of the stub wings and powerful engine of that Waco airplane. We were impressed before we took our orientation flight and bruised and battered after we took it. He could do things with that airplane most of us had never imagined. He was sadistic. He was a fiend. He set the tone for our elementary learning when we climbed in that open cockpit for the first time. Among other things, he hollered, "Is your seat belt tight?"

"Yes, sir!"

"I mean real tight?"

"Yes, sir."

"All right, here we go. Now you can follow along with your hand gently on the stick. And I do mean gently. Put your feet very lightly on the pedals. And I do mean very lightly. I don't want to feel any pressure of your hands or feet until I tell you." He was threatening enough and intimidating enough that I thought it was a pretty good time to quit the whole program and go fishing. But I

36

didn't get the chance. He pushed enough throttle to race down to takeoff position and spun onto the runway. As we spun sideways, he gave it full throttle and away we went. What power. My head banged the back of the seat. My hand banged the stick, and my instructor banged back sideways so hard the stick hit the inside of both my knees about three times each. These tactics got my attention.

The takeoff was noisy and rough, but once we got airborne, all was smooth. My instructor quit hollering as we gained some altitude. Over the Bitterroot Valley I looked out to enjoy the beauty of the land below, the mountains ahead, and the prospect of a nice, gentle cruise about the countryside. Boy, this was living. But it was not to be for very long. Once we were out of sight of the airport those mountains ahead suddenly changed places with the land below. At the same time, my elbows were over my head, my knees were up by my chin, the gaspord tube was over my helmet, and the dirt and dust from the floor fell up to the sky—or was it down toward the ground? The most important thing to me was that I didn't fall out. My butt was about six inches off the parachute I was supposed to be sitting on, and my goggles fell down on my upper lip. But I had already learned something. When your seat belt is supposed to be very tight, it had better be very, very tight. We were flat upside down, and only my Saint Christopher medal kept me from falling out. It was only a few seconds before the engine began to sputter and die, because those carburetors were not meant to function upside down, but it was almost too long for me. I'd gotten the message that the wheels were up on the top of the plane and my instructor and I had our heads pointed toward Mother Earth.

He hollered through the tube for me to grab the controls and "straighten 'er out." I had an idea what should be done but didn't know how to overcome the gravity on my hands and feet. I just hung on for dear life. He let the plane slop around until the weight of the engine and slow speed forward put the nose down toward earth and we went into a spin. That was better—I'd done that in a

Cub—but I'm sure I didn't recover from this spin by myself. He must have helped. There had been no time for airsickness, but had it happened I knew the penalty. If you puked you cleaned it up real good. I didn't get sick. In fact, when my heart began beating again for sure, I decided I liked this kind of flying. It was fun. I became a challenge to this instructor and he must have accepted me some, because he taught me a bunch about lifesaving maneuvers and a little about aerobatics that was not in the manual.

Phase II in that Waco went by too fast. The things we were learning in ground school were the practical parts of being a pilot beyond just flying the aircraft. Ground school included such basics as: how to deal with other air traffic; how to navigate from maps, railroads, highways, section fence lines, and mountain ranges (remember, is the principal mountain on your left or on your right?); how to read the weather; cross-country flying; forced landings without power; airport rules and etiquette; and, of course, record keeping. In the air we became a bit macho when we got to go around to different airports without an instructor. We could even charge gas to Johnson's if we needed some. Flying beside some black weather "learned" us some places not to go. And when we did stick our noses into thunderstorm activity, if it bounced you around pretty hard and made you pucker up a bit it was a firm reminder of your limitations and gave you respect for the power of a storm.

I was fortunate to have completed that phase in the minimum time required. Then I could spend a few weeks in the aircraft or in classes I liked or just hanging around the airport. Not having to repeat any classes gave me some much needed confidence. Hot spit!

During the spring of 1941 an examination board from the air arm of the U.S. Navy went visiting the schools that had CPT programs. They came by the University of Montana. Because I liked the idea of wearing those white dress uniforms, I went to meet them. There was no problem with my written test, no problem with my experience qualification (private pilot's license), and no problem with the physical, I thought, until the very last thing, when the dentist noticed I had a two-place bridge. "You cannot fly navy aircraft with a two-place bridge. One, yes. Two, no." I had been rejected. It was a real blow.

Not long after that, a similar team came by representing the Army Air Corps. They only had five or six aspirants show up to inquire about the Air Corps or wanting to make application to join up. The Air Corps team was a good PR bunch, and we were all convinced that the Air Corps was the way to go. I showed their leader, a mighty major, my application and results from the navy team. He hollered over to one of his guys, "Have you ever heard of disqualifying an applicant on only the fact that he has a two-place bridge?"

"No, sir, never have."

"Here, run this man through. We want George as an aviation cadet." So all I had to do was wait for my first set of official orders telling me when and where to report.

Chapter 5
Military Flight Training

The summer of 1941 was a very relaxed but exciting period. Exciting because I knew those orders would be coming soon and because the exact location that I would go for flight training was unknown, and also because it was a good chance to learn to water-ski. No reason to go to college—what if I had to leave on short notice? No reason to work very much in the store—I'd soon be making a living in the military.

And there was Bob Anderson. He was a speedboat owner, could even build one if he had to. He had recently talked his mother into buying a residential lot on the shore of Flathead Lake right near the golf course in Polson, so why shouldn't I help him build a summer house on that dandy lot? We didn't let the demands of house building keep us from doing quite a bit of waterskiing. Bob was a lot better than I, but it was just as much fun to run the boat. Bob had made a big, long set of skis out of cedar, so they were very lightweight. His boat-building heritage told him the skis should have a keel so there would be more control in the water. Long, narrow, light skis with an old pair of tennis shoes fastened about midway and a keel about one inch deep made a right fancy set with a large amount of show-off potential. We practiced a lot, and I must say we got to be pretty fair skiers, too. That was a brand-new lake sport and not much of it was seen, but slow boats out sightseeing in Polson Bay got to see a lot of us. Bob's boat was a good one. It was fast and it roared "real good."

Came some kind of a holiday, probably Fourth of July, to Polson, and a lot of people were going to be there to see and participate in all kinds of water sports. We'd heard that the local chamber of commerce had hired a couple of water-skiers to come over from Sandpoint, Idaho, and put on an exhibition. Naturally, Bob and I wouldn't take that sleeping in the shade. When the exhibitors arrived, we were surprised to notice their skis were dead flat on the bottom and about six inches wide. We'd never seen anything like that. Our one pair was keeled and about three inches wide. Well, those showoffs raced around the bay for about half an hour, did a few tricks, fell down a few times, and then announced the big event. They'd concocted a floating ramp that went up at about a forty-degree angle and was about five feet wide. The rise from the water was about ten feet long and five feet high. The main feature was for one of them to ski around in front of the stands and then at full-bore (and it was a fast boat, but no better than ours) approach and go up that ramp and fly through the air, land on the water, and ski off. He did it. The folks liked it so much he came back and did it again. I suppose they then got paid, the exhibitors I mean, and headed home.

That was too much for Anderson. The program was over, so he said, "I'm gonna do a little going around and show the people we have as much local talent as they brought in from out of state. Go around the bay in front of the stands, but go fast. I'll do a single ski once in a while, but don't slow down."

I did as I was told, and our boat was great. It went faster than those guys' and made more noise, and Anderson really looked good. Didn't fall down at all. The spray he'd make on a big fast S maneuver was a sight to behold. We stopped a few minutes to let him rest. I guess a challenge must have bit him, because he said, "I'm gonna try that jump. Go around once and pass close to the ramp, and on the second round I'll take the jump. But hit it hard and fast."

We went around like a bat outta Hades! On the second pass we were moving about as fast as any boat had ever gone on that lake, so I headed just next to the ramp. Bob hit that incline right in the middle. The next thing I saw was Bob coming off the top going ass-over-teakettle. He had half of a ski on one foot and no ski at all on the other. He hit the water so hard, going so fast, I though he'd drown and be killed besides. A head did pop above water, so I pulled alongside to help him into the boat. He didn't appear to be physically hurt. He said, "Get me to hell outta here. Everyone will be laughing at me. It was those damned skis. Because of the keel on the bottom, when I hit the ramp my knees popped out sideways, and I was wrecked before I got halfway up." Another design theory had been scrapped. From then on all water-skis were flat-bottomed. Nobody laughed at Bob.

Finally a communiqué arrived from the Air Corps. It said I would be assigned to the Gulf Coast Training Command and would be receiving orders from them telling me when, where, and how to report.

Kelly Field, Texas. I had heard about it for some time and knew that it was one of the premier Army Air Corps training schools. They didn't mention that it was currently used only as a preflight center and no flight training would be done there by this new type Air Corps people. We would receive only ground school instruction about army discipline, procedures, discipline, history, discipline, and hazing. So what? We had a title: Aviation Cadet. It was enough to make a young guy happy.

Only a few things stand out about that time at Kelly. One was that as an underclassman you always had to run, not walk, when outside, unless ordered not to. When meeting an upperclassman you got about three steps to stop, get out of his way, back against a building or anything solid, and look straight ahead in the most rigid "brace" you could muster. If you didn't brace fast enough or hard enough, the high-and-mighty upperclassman could give you some loud instructions about almost anything, but especially about your stupidity and unworthiness, all about six inches away from being nose to nose. The word *scum* had already been invented, so I tried my best to remember that only a very few weeks ago that rotten guy had also been scum.

Pistol and rifle practice was interesting, but we'd have been better off without the training, because we didn't really want to be partially qualified to be footsoldiers in case we got "washed out" of flying school. Later, in the combat zone, we always carried our .45 pistols, and we had two Thompson submachine guns in the airplane. I suppose this was in case we ever ran into a battleship and decided to sink it single-handed.

Wake-up call was from a real live early-riser bugler. Cadets had twenty-seven minutes to get up, shave (if qualified), make the bed, shower, and be in formation and ready for roll call. Two seconds late meant one tour. One tour was fifty-five minutes walking back and forth in full military uniform, with rifle, in front of the base administration building. Those tours were available to be paid off only on your otherwise free time. It was not conducive to good mental or physical health to have too many of them.

Mealtime was usually a good time of day, because it broke exactly on time whatever you were being harassed with at that moment. Every mealtime was good. The mess halls were immaculate. The food was very good and it was plentiful, if you got to eat it. The upperclassmen got to eat, but the underclassmen were subject to unprovoked and ridiculous hazing. Two instances come to mind.

One time the tables were set for twelve cadets, alternating one upperclassman with one lowly underclassman around the table. The food was then passed around so that the uppers could help themselves to all they wanted of the choicest pieces and casually begin to eat, while using up precious minutes of our allotted mealtime allowance. When the bell sounded, you stopped right then. If your fork was in midair it went back to the plate and you stood up at attention.

Sometimes an unlucky under would be just beginning to eat his meal when a diabolical upper would casually call out his name, just for the hell of it: "Cadet Murphy!" That meant that Murphy had to brace immediately. Fork or spoon on the table right now. Into a hard brace right now. Shoulders back. Eyes straight ahead. Hands at your sides reaching for the floor. "Sound off, Murphy!" meant that Murphy was to recite: "Aviator Cadet Murphy, sir. My hometown is Hardrock, Arkansas. My college was Riverside State University. My fraternity was Alpha Beta Zilch" (or whatever applied to the hungry cadet).

"Well, Cadet Murphy, that is a good place to be from. What were you famous for in Hardrock?"

At that point, as the others ate on, Murphy would have to come up with some wild imaginary tale in an attempt to make the upperclassmen laugh. If they didn't laugh, which they seldom did, the uppers would groan, ridicule, and let the unfortunate victim know that he didn't amount to much. On the other hand, if he could make the uppers laugh (unders were forbidden to laugh), it was an unwritten rule that the cadet would then be exempt from further hazing. Much planning went into preparation by the unders on various ways to be famous. One guy from the U of Montana, a Sigma Chi, foolishly chose to respond with one of those preplanned answers. At that time, the upper class was being transitioned into blue uniforms from the army tan and gray. Upon hearing, "And what were you famous for up in that cold country?" the brace-laden response was, "I was a manufacturer of blue condoms. I got very rich selling them in Texas."

"That's unusual, but how could you become famous selling them only in Texas?"

"Well, sir, this seemed to be the only place where all the pricks are dressed in blue."

All hell broke loose. The underclassmen laughed and hooted; the uppers got flushed and mad. Fortunately, the bell rang and that situation ended. That clever cadet did not get much to eat the next couple meals, because you can't eat while in a brace. Mercifully, the table "head" acknowledged some lad had laughed. I was not hazed anymore.

A second hazing incident that I shall never forget involved Harry Hamilton Webster. He was braced for asking someone to pass the grape jelly. The request was okay. The problem was that Harry asked while his mouth was still stuffed with potatoes and gravy. He had to stay braced while the uppers went through an analysis of what makes it jelly and what makes it jam. Harry got quite stressed, because he didn't dare swallow. He was braced so hard he could hardly breathe. Almost everyone else at the table was chuckling and grinning, because the whole world knew you should not ask for jelly when your mouth was full. Finally the explosion. Harry could hold it no longer. He spewed potatoes and gravy across the table, onto the shirt of one of his best cadet buddies, and dripped some on his own necktie. The uppers weren't that hard on him, though; he only missed a meal or two, because a day later we became upper-classmen.

As upperclassmen the heat was off. Instead of obeying rules most of the time, we were now enforcing the existing ones and even making a few new ones so the regiment would have something to remember us by. We weren't as hung up on the chicken stuff as were our predecessors, but we were sticklers on the matter of discipline. In my opinion, we actually got better results and accomplished more by leaning toward being leaders instead of dictators. Besides, we didn't have any West Pointers, as our predecessors did. But we did have Tom Harmon, one of the greatest football players of all time.

The war effort seemed to be going along smoothly. The military was expanding rapidly with the draft in full swing. Factories were working around-the-clock. Roosevelt made it possible to have a new outhouse on every farm at half-price. The average citizen seemed to have pride in America.

Then: Sunday, December 7, 1941. The Japanese made a devastating attack against the United States while our defense forces were still snoozing on an early, glamorous Honolulu morning. Pearl Harbor was wrecked. Our Pacific fleet was almost totally destroyed. The Japanese attack planes had hardly been touched, and the command forces in our army and navy didn't even know where the attackers came from or where they went. A few days later, our bases in the Philippines were rendered helpless. MacArthur headed for Australia. (Thank God.)

The embarrassment, the disgrace, and the terrible casualties were intended to, and could have, destroyed our resolve. But that didn't happen. The American people rose in unison, raised the flag, and seemed to say, "Let's get with it." After all, we had some aircraft carriers in the Pacific that had been at sea and consequently were untouched by the Pearl Harbor raid, MacArthur was headed for Australia, and we had a new bunch of aviation cadets down in Texas ready to come on line. We had plenty of navy in the Atlantic, and Liberty ships were doing their job under the protection of that navy in keeping the European forces supplied with men and equipment. Not only did the mood of the nation change, it changed for the better, all the way down to the aviation cadets at Kelly Field, Texas.

Primary Flight Training—Chickasha, Oklahoma

There were no wasted days in moving these Kelly Field cadets to the brand-new school in Chickasha. We left one day, got moved into the proper barracks on the next day, and were scheduled for duty the following day. The army seemed to have suddenly become very efficient, from a logistical standpoint. Perhaps it was the sense of urgency that set the tone of "get it done rapidly, but get it done properly" and got everyone cooperating. The flight instructors were brand-new second lieutenants. Some lacked instructor experience but knew they had the responsibility of choosing the best of the litter from this bunch of new cadets who were to get their first exposure to military flight indoctrination. The instructors could neither pamper nor hold over any trainee who lacked any of the required physical or mental traits demanded by the rigorous program. About 50 percent of that primary flight class were washed out. This was a terrible blow to each of the cadets whose plan to become a pilot was dashed or seriously set back.

Our airplanes were low-wing Fairchild PT-19s. They had two open cockpits, yellow wings, and a blue body. The PT-19 was a streamlined craft with a 175-horsepower engine. The airplane was easy to fly and was capable of spins, rolls, and stalls. But on the first introduction to the plane with an instructor, I wasn't too sure it would be fun.

"This," the instructor said, "is an airplane. I expect you to learn real fast just what the plane will do under your guidance. You will be handling the controls unless I tell you otherwise. You'd better learn fast, because half of my job is to wash out those that don't learn or those that don't pay attention or anyone who violates safety rules."

I thought I had another son of a gun for an instructor, but it wasn't so. He and most of those young instructors were anxious to make good pilots out of all of us. My prior CPT hours at Missoula gave me a leg up, because most of the instructors were not very experienced. We flew some every day and had ground school also. Except Sunday. My check ride at about the one-third point was easy. After just a few minutes in the air, the instructor gave me a simulated forced landing, but my mean old former instructor had done that many times. After him, I nearly always knew the wind direction, from smoke, dust, or other, and had learned to constantly look for a reasonably level and tree-free spot within gliding distance in case of a real forced landing. During the check ride, I already knew the wind direction and had a field picked out, so I made the necessary turns and headed toward the field. We squared away into the wind. We went down, down, until we were about ten feet off the ground.

The field didn't look too smooth, and I got plenty worried that the instructor was not going to push throttle and take us back in the air. At five feet, three feet, and even one foot, he had still not goosed it. I was ready to panic, but he was the one who had pulled back the throttle and it was his job to get us flying. I just sweated. It was hard to keep my hand away from the throttle, and I wasn't brave enough to just "let 'er land." What if it tore off the landing gear? He could wash me out.

The wheels hit the dirt. There were plenty of bangs and bounces, and then he throttled it full bore. He got us about ten feet off the ground and then said, "Take me home." We hadn't been up fifteen minutes, so I suspected he was about to give me my walking papers. I took us home and landed the plane. We got out without a word and walked to Operations. He told me to put my parachute away and come into the office. I felt mighty low, but I knew his word was law. If he said I was through as a cadet, I was through. Shattered dreams. And not yet one-third of the way through primary training.

"Well," he said, "that took some guts to not touch the throttle. You remembered the rules. Your instructor says you are passing all your flights in good shape. Unless he tells me something to the contrary, you won't be needing another check ride and you will be graduating with your class and going on to basic flight training." *Wow!* I could thank my rotten old flight instructor from CPT for my success though.

Basic Flight Training—Enid, Oklahoma

The planes were Vultee BT-13s. They were called vibrators because they shook so much. They were quite a bit heavier than anything I had been in and had a good Pratt and Whitney engine with more horsepower than any other training planes I had experienced so far. There was an upper class of cadets here, but they had limited time for hazing and probably didn't care to participate. In a few weeks we became upperclassmen, and we practically let hazing die out during our time. We spent a good portion of our air time flying at night. We flew rain or shine. There were a lot of springtime thunderstorms, especially at night, and we were expected to learn two very important things. We were to "remember what you learned in weather class and don't let a big, bad thunderstorm get you." They also warned us, "If you've been tossed around and frightened because of lightning and rough air, still remember how to get back to base." The instructors thought it very funny when the poor sweating student would have to ask for help locating home base. We had no radio direction finder, and occasionally a student, flying solo at night, would land at some lighted field that wasn't his own. Appropriate ridicule and punishment were always available.

We had our first taste of formation flying at this stage. One of the instructor's favorite tricks involved having four planes echelon right. The cadet pilots would be lazing around the sky with the instructor encouraging each student to keep it "tucked in real close." Then he would head into a harmless cloud bank. If the number-two guy (on his wing) was tucked in close, he could follow the leader quite easily. But often number two gave a little space, out of fright, and then number three would give some more. By then, numbers four and five couldn't see anyone. The leader's gentle left turn would bring him out of the clouds, often alone or sometimes with one student or two, but rarely all four. He would then head off in another direction and usually go down to ground level with the ones that had hung onto him. He would radio the other lost sheep to come find him, especially if they wanted to get home in time for supper.

Every day something was learned that might save our lives later on. Tuck it in. Be alert. Be confident. Be disciplined. Be gentle on the controls. Each time we flew, these reminders became more second nature and easier than the time before.

49

Advanced Flying School—Lake Charles, Louisiana

The choice advanced school in the Gulf Coast training area was beautiful Lake Charles. Water, green grass, a vibrant city, palatial homes, and an air of hospitality made this period a far cry from the prior assignments. We cadets had matured a lot in those few short weeks. The odds suddenly seemed to assure us that we could become partially qualified aircraft pilots, gentlemen and officers in our chosen branch of the service. Unfortunately, about 30 percent of our advanced class were destined to be washed out even at this late stage of training.

The airplanes were North American AT-6s (the same as the navy SN-J). They had a 650-horsepower Pratt and Whitney engine and were two-seat tandem, with an enclosed cockpit. But most exciting of all, a .30 caliber machine gun was mounted on the fuselage just in front of the pilot's seat. The machine gun was programmed to fire through the rotating propeller blades.

That larger, more powerful engine made a much more distinctive sound (really a rumble), more grand than the washing-machine types we had previously flown. The AT-6 took off at a higher speed, could get to a higher altitude much quicker, and cruised faster than other trainers. It was heavy and much more sensitive to controls, so it felt like we really had a powerful machine under us. Landing was not too hard, but it was very important to remember to lower the landing gear before touching down. Since this was the first plane any of us had flown that had retractable gear, it took a new form of concentration when preparing to land. I recall only one occasion in our class when a cadet landed without wheels. That meant immediate washout for him and enough fear in the rest of us so that we didn't forget.

The AT-6 had another characteristic. For the inattentive pilot who had touched down and was most of the way through his rollout, torque, wind, or a slight turn could suddenly move the in-motion center of gravity out from directly behind the propeller. If the pilot didn't feel that situation soon enough to correct it, the plane would, quick as a flash, go into a horizontal spin for up to a full turn, right there in front of God and everyone else. That was called a ground loop. It's like a car turning end to end on ice. Not a washout offense, but the instructors took a very dim view of it. Naturally, I never did one.

We did a lot of interesting things in the AT-6: Close formation (and I do mean close, but not as dangerous as it looks), low-level attack, hiding behind hedgerows along the canals, simulated attacks on freight trains, and flying over the cotton fields with maybe ten feet of clearance. But all that was without any ammunition. I guess we were like little kids playing with popguns.

However, about midway through· we got to go to the Alamagordo firing range just off the coast of Texas. There the AT-6 guns were loaded with live ammo and we got to shoot at targets being towed behind a plane, ground targets, and even a moving target on water. The way our effectiveness was evaluated was by the number of holes in the target with each trainee's assigned color showing; the ammunition had been dipped in various color compounds. The instructors always had their little joke. "Anyone who shoots down a tow plane has to clean the latrines that night." Tow plane duty was not considered a high-priority assignment.

There was a trick we liked to do with the hand-held microphone. We'd let the microphone with its attached flexible cord just rest in its clamp. Then we would hold our hands in the vicinity of the mike about six or ten inches away, with fingers and thumb opened, ready to hold the mike. Certain flight maneuvers would change the gravitational pull, causing the mike to leave its cradle and float around in the air like a Hindu pipe player's snake. It would go up or down or left or right according to the way the pilot changed direction. The game was to let the gravity phenomenon put the mike handle gently twixt our thumb and fingers so we could then press the button and make a radio call. Just how that helped us become better pilots I don't know, but it was something that wasn't in the book, and fun besides.

At this stage in our training it seemed that anything less than perfection, or at least competence, would result in washout. However, we had one guy in advanced who was a constant danger to be around when he was in the air. Nothing great on the ground either. How he got this far I never knew. He couldn't fly formation, jumpy, jerky, in and out. He couldn't land without a bounce or two or three. He had the lowest score at gunnery practice, and he just generally was not smooth. It was an unwritten rule that in formation flying we'd put this fellow in last position; tail end Charley, it's called. Regardless of who was flight leader, if we got into any weather or were just playing around in big cumulus clouds or if we had restricted visibility, the leader would turn away from our tail end Charley. The leader never aimed straight ahead or toward our weak link's position. He was a collision just waiting to happen. But for some reason he never got washed out. Maybe his father was a big shot. He did graduate but was never given a specific assignment. Never did hear more of him, but always feared he might show up too close for comfort. That would include the same theater of operations.

About two weeks before our anticipated graduation day from advanced, we were given a questionnaire regarding our preference choices for type of aircraft we would prefer to fly when assigned to a tactical unit. The army always wants to know what your choices are so that they can assign you to something else. As far as I know, just about all of our small class of twenty-five or thirty put their preferences this way: first choice: fighters; second choice: heavy bombardment; third choice: medium bombardment; others: none. From that time on, we talked fighter planes.

On our last day as aviation cadets, we and the administrative officers of the school were invited to a beautiful home on the shore of Lake Charles for an elaborate barbecue. We cadets were all quite nervous, never having been on a lawn that large, nor having seen a table piled so high with every imaginable kind of good food. The hosts were very cordial, so we soon relaxed and talked about how it would always be this classy when we got to be officers. And that would be tomorrow.

The graduation ceremonies were held in the recreation hall at the school at 10:00 A.M. sharp. We sat in the few chairs while the base commander made some appropriate remarks and then asked the adjutant to read off the names, with rank and assignments. Being alphabetically inferior, W, I had a long wait till he got to my name. Prior to my turn, there had been several called "with rank of warrant officer" and some "with rank of second lieutenant," so I had to sweat out fate again. I didn't want to be a warrant officer. Most of the assignments so far had been to units and bases unknown, so I began to feel I'd luck out and get fighter pilot after all. Finally (it was only a short time, but it seemed long to me), "Wamsley, George Walter, Jr., second lieutenant, report to First Troop Carrier Command, Stout Field, Indianapolis, Indiana." The base CO pinned on my wings, and I was an officer and a gentleman. But what was First Troop Carrier Command? Never had heard of it.

Troop Carrier Command—Indianapolis, Indiana

The traditional thirty-day delay en route at this period in the military was supposed to give the new officer a chance to spend his pay, buy new uniforms, and brag about his new status. Again, however, the time element got squeezed with notice to "proceed forthwith by any means available to Stout Field, Indianapolis, Indiana." Most locals at Indianapolis didn't know that Stout had become a military base. A minimum number of troop carrier personnel were doing what they could to take care of the incoming second lieutenants. Thanks to a government checkbook they could arrange food, lodging, and housekeeping for the few (probably twenty in the next three weeks) army hot-dog, flying-type pilots who showed up ready to do their thing.

One of the few planes at that large airport was an American Airlines DC-3 with red, white, and blue stripes running from nose to tail. The large red lettering, American Airlines, on the shining aluminum fuselage skin made it a beautiful sight. A good-looking Army Air Corps boss-type person picked four of us, had us sign in, and before any other welcoming ceremonies said, "Come with me." We walked out on the tarmac, and he said, "I'm Captain [whatever]. Sorry to be in such a hurry, but we are just trying to get some flight transition under way and I want you to meet your keeper for the next couple of weeks." We walked up to that DC-3, where there stood a fine-looking elderly gentleman, at least fifty years old. He was dressed in the glamorous attire of a veteran airline pilot, with four stripes sewn on in various places that indicated he was a senior aircraft commander.

"Gentlemen, introduce yourselves to Captain Groendyke. He is one of the top pilots flying DC-3 aircraft today. You are most fortunate to have him teach you, in a very few days, what it took him several years to learn. Listen up real good."

Captain Groendyke asked, "Any of you ever been in a passenger airline cockpit?"

Since none of the four of us had, the captain invited us up. What a shock. The back half of the cabin had cushion seats and backs in bright red and dark blue. The front half of the passenger cabin obviously had four bunks on each side of the aisle, one over and one under, with deep purple velvet curtains from ceiling to floor. It was what I would have imagined would be the look of an expensive French whorehouse. That was American Airlines' version of first-class sleeper service from coast to coast.

This was a training plane? The cockpit was small and crowded with gear, radios, shelves, and instruments on every side, above and below. How could a guy learn all about all of this? Besides, you were sitting about fifteen feet above ground, so how would you know where the landing wheels were?

Captain Groendyke was great. He was soft-spoken, friendly, easygoing, thorough, and sympathetic, and he had a sense of humor under that stern Germanic countenance. How could he have both? He had each of the four of us sit in the pilot's seat while he explained the rudimentary workings of the "office." We were fascinated. It was overwhelming. So much to learn in so little time. He reiterated, "It took me several years sitting in the copilot's seat before I was even permitted to attempt a landing or a takeoff. Each of you will have at least five hours in the pilot's seat before I send you on your way. Sometimes you will be in the copilot's seat while I talk to the pilot over your shoulders. Sometimes I will ride copilot. Listen; look; learn; ask questions. First is safety first. If it doesn't feel right, let's talk about it. We will fly together for four hours at a time. Each of you will fly pilot for about an hour while the other three observe or fly copilot. Have a good night's sleep. See you tomorrow at Operations at 0800."

Egad. As of now we didn't know where to sleep or eat or go to the bathroom.

In spite of his misgivings, the captain was good to his word. The instruments began to make sense. We got a better idea about how far the landing gear was below our behind. The plane's two engines became one, especially when he would simulate fire in one engine or a bad prop or a mysterious malfunction. But those two Wright 1100 engines were the best. They were easy to start. After a few pops and bangs and a bunch of white smoke, they'd kick off. Since this was our first experience with two engines, it was necessary to remember to have the brakes locked or at least pushed hard down by foot to keep the plane from turning in a circle when we got the first engine going. It was easy to taxi, if there wasn't any wind blowing the tail crosswise. More power on one engine and the gentle application of one brake would keep you going where you wanted to go, provided you knew where you wanted to go to get in takeoff position. Just for fun, the captain started us out by having the pilot do everything on the ground: keep the airplane moving, guide it, throttle it, brake it, talk to the tower, watch all instruments, and not run into other planes or buildings. After a time or two, the copilot would do his share of those functions, and then later it would all become second nature. But the responsibility remained the pilot's.

Supposedly we had learned the basics of airport protocol, like how to communicate with the tower and other routine procedures before takeoff. This phase was just to be a checkout in this type of plane. Because of the size, weight, multiengines, and number of instruments, this task seemed awesome.

But it all fell into place quite rapidly. The captain talked; we listened. We ran the throttles, hollered, "Gearup!" to the copilot, indicated flaps up or down with a casual flip of a thumb, trimmed the tabs, synchronized the engines, and tried to remember where the field was. For the first few landings and takeoffs, we'd follow through on the controls while the captain made the moves. All too soon came the request. "Now you take her around and I'll follow." A two- or three-bounce landing, usually too short on the runway or too far down, would be finished by the captain. Each time the landing was a little more graceful, and all too soon, I think, I heard: "Okay, George, get in the pilot's seat. Jack, you're the copilot. You other two guys stand behind and watch. I'll be about halfway down the runway. I'll be off on the edge. Don't run over me. If I give you crossed arms, pull to a stop. If I wave you on, don't stop. Just give her the gas and go around again till I sign you to stop."

I know he said to himself, under his breath, "And God help you, it can't be done with only five hours of time at the controls." But he opened the door, got out, shook his head, and waved me away. We got up okay, got the gear up, flew around the landing pattern, got the gear down, touched down, and rolled a short distance. Then there was that beautiful sight—old Groendyke waving his arm—go again, go again. After four or five reasonably successful landings, he had me stop. In the cockpit we switched positions, and the other guys went through the same procedure. After we had each made our landings, Groendyke called us in. He had a great big grin and a hug for each of us. He kept saying, "I didn't think you could do it. I didn't think you could do it." It was a good day. We had not crashed the airplane.

I didn't see the captain much after that, but he did take us all on some real instrument condition flights in order that we could be qualified instrument pilots, but just barely. He told me he had talked the flight transition training officer into giving the student pilots a little more time hereafter before making them go solo. That was a very good idea.

We all got quite a bit of time in the Link Trainer. That is a fabulous flight simulator that makes you feel and act like you are in the middle of a storm, with no way to save your life except to analyze the situation by reading and believing the instruments. The Link instructor could put you in a critical situation by making the instruments tell you that you were almost upside down or going into a spin. The pilot either figured out how to recover or, theoretically, crashed. It was always good to finish a session and step out on a solid floor. At worst, we got a scolding from the instructor, but we were alive.

There are two kinds of weather conditions. One is CAVU; that means Ceiling And Visibility Unlimited. The second condition is bad weather, which requires that a pilot be "instrument-rated." A pilot with an instrument rating has been trained to handle reasonably bad weather. The tower or operations people can tell you if the weather is fit or unfit for you to fly. A pilot qualified for a green clearance card can tell the tower or operations people whether he chooses to fly, or not, in adverse weather. By the time we returned from overseas we were all green card–qualified. And we had learned the hard way.

Out of twenty-two days at Stout, I flew on twenty days. Must have gotten two Sundays off. Hard to believe it was just about a year before this when I had helped Bob Anderson break in his water skis on Flathead Lake, in the summer of 1941.

Troop Carrier Command—Florence, South Carolina

By the summer of 1942, we left Stout for Florence, South Carolina. I don't recall if we took planes along or just got unloaded there. The place was a little, insignificant airport with very few buildings. I think the great powers were organizing a couple of squadrons, because there were some radio operators and a few crew chiefs, in addition to a few pilots. The management worked out of a small residence near the field. We practiced some three-plane formation flying in C-47s where we simulated dropping parachute troops. That means when you approach the jump area, you slow the plane down to almost stall speed, pull the nose up some more, and push the button that rings the bell in the main cabin that prompts the jump master to holler, "Go!" He hits the first paratrooper on the behind, and out the door the first jumper goes. Number two is by then in the door and gets his hit and is out the door. For deployment, their chutes are fastened to a static cable running along the ceiling, which opens the chute when the jumper is about fifteen feet out the door. The trooper does carry a reserve chute that he can open by hand, pulling a rip cord, but the second chute is seldom needed. A string of twenty jumpers could evacuate the plane in about thirty seconds. They had better be out, because by then the pilot would be just at stall speed and he'd jam the nose downward. This pushes the tail upward, which makes the people and all loose equipment get banged about because of the sudden change in gravity. With all this going on, the pilot is still supposed to have his plane in his nice little formation. It looks much prettier from the ground.

Sure enough. After a few days of that kind of practice, without ever dropping a real live paratrooper, we got the word to head for Pope Field, Fort Bragg—home of the already famous Eighty-second Airborne. The Eighty-second was, and still is, the best-looking, tallest-standing, most disciplined bunch of soldiers in the U.S. military. They are alert, strong, intelligent, and proud.

By the time most of the C-47s from the various troop carrier fields in the southern states arrived at Pope, the Eighty-second guys were in their proper places with their chutes and ready to climb aboard. The Eighty-second Airborne Command had organized the exercise so well that the thirty or so C-47s were assigned positions by threes, handed a few written instructions, given a command radio frequency, and started loading the jumpers. Most of us had never dropped a paratrooper or even flown in a formation that size, but by then we knew we had better do it right. A bunch of high-ranking individuals from Washington, military and civilian, were in the VIP spectators' section. The radio instructions were clear, concise, understandable, and absolutely not subject to discussion. Three by three we got into position and off the ground without serious incident. We got into formation without too much trouble and flew toward the drop zone in less than perfect formation, but we held our assigned altitude well enough that we didn't drive through the guys ahead who had already jumped. Collectively, we made the prettiest picture of the largest practice jump yet attempted by the Eighty-second. As I recall, there were over 500 jumpers. Secretary of State Cordell Hull was in the audience. He reported it as a perfect demonstration and wrote that everyone involved had "done good." I never saw the memo, so I don't know the exact language.

Dropping those paratroopers and observing the type gear they took along on this seriously simulated live mission was probably when we learned what Troop Carrier Command really meant. The troopers jumped with an automatic rifle and real live ammunition, full water canteens, rations for ten days, a sixteen-inch machete, blackface, heavy gloves, mess gear, a prayer book, and usually a picture of their loved ones. The flight group that I was assigned to was picked to be located and used where the dirty work was going on, amongst the enemy, up front, with the troops.

59

With all due respect, we were not Air Transport Command. Some of the more uncouth among us even went so far as to define the ATC, affectionately of course, as "Army for Terrified Civilians" or "Allergic To Combat." We did think it would have been better to be in ATC until we figured out we'd always be lugging along dress uniforms, razors, soap, and clean underwear and of course we'd be drinking free drinks and eating those fine meals from menus in fancy officers' clubs or per-diem-paid elegant hotels. Besides, there might be times we'd have to dance with girls we didn't even know at some of those optional (but compulsory) "The Commander requests your attendance at this evening's soiree . . . "

Naw, we'd be better off with the flies, mosquitoes, mud, and sweat of some steamy jungle far from civilization.

While at Florence, we did some kind of flying every day and gradually gathered together some brand-new C-47s. A trip to pick up a new airplane from the Mobile, Alabama, air depot was another indication of what might be in store. On that trip, I had a staff sergeant copilot. The staff sergeant pilots were fully qualified pilots but had trained at different schools. After landing, the air depot operations officer invited me to have some lunch at the officers' club. My copilot and I followed him a few steps before he said, "Hey, he can't eat with us."

That was a new one on me. I said, "I bet he can. Where is the officers' club? If he doesn't eat with me, I don't eat, and I doubt if your CO would care to hear about that."

We went to the club and got a fine lunch. The sergeant had better manners than either of us. That was a first, but it was not the last time for me to close one of the overdone gaps between enlisted men and officers.

The new planes had a cargo door large enough to accommodate a jeep or a wheeled mortar launcher or to roll out fifty-gallon drums of gasoline, which we did a lot of later on. There were fold-down metal benches that would seat twenty-four butts. A static line ran along the ceiling, which must have meant paratroopers.

New radios and a seat for the operator in a dinky compartment just behind the pilot's looked good. But there was no place for the pilot's friend, the crew chief (mechanic). He was usually so nervous he hovered between the pilots and studied the gauges. Lots of the crew chiefs liked to fly the copilot seat, and they liked to handle the controls. There was a new device called an IFF, which meant Identify: Friend or Foe. I never did know how it worked, nor did I ever hear a foe call in. When friends talked to us, they did it by radio, so maybe the IFF was something extra.

How did we tinkle? Wet? Pee-pee? Urinate? A convenient small rubber relief tube was just under each pilot's seat. Successful engagement with the proper part of the pilot's anatomy would carry the liquid to the great outdoors and down on the farms or cities below—or maybe it would evaporate. Another innovative aspect of this aircraft was brackets just beside the cabin door that held a weapon clearly marked: ONE ONLY THOMPSON SUBMACHINE GUN.

Back at Florence, a new designation was posted. My flight group was to be the Thirty-third Troop Carrier Squadron. The first people assigned were crews made up of a pilot, a copilot, a crew chief, and a radio operator. Thirteen such crews coincided with the number of aircraft allocated under the Table of Organization sent down from Washington. I don't recall that there was a designated commanding officer at that time but it wasn't long before those thirteen planes and crews were ordered to head for Sacramento, to be outfitted with gear and supplies for extended overseas assignment. I sure hoped we wouldn't get a bunch of cold-weather clothing. The rumor mill had suggested that Alaska was to become a major in-transit ferry-type operation.

Twelve of our planes were dispatched by some route to Sacramento. One—namely mine—was ordered to proceed to Bolling Field, Washington, D.C., to pick up some mysterious lightweight packages important to our proposed mission. No definite information. No clues as to what the packages might contain. They were essential enough that an inexperienced pilot could be sent into that beehive of airplanes at Washington Airport. It was the first time I fully realized I was expendable, along with my crew. We did get on the ground, were directed to a parking place, and were met by a car with driver. After we ordered some fuel, we were driven off through a maze of streets to the office of the person I was to meet. I expected at least a general, but the nice second lieutenant said, "Oh sure, I've got some new kind of astral guides for you guys going into the South Pacific. But that is a secret. Don't you say a word. You can use them at night if you are over a large body of water and can't get any radio contact." It verified one thing, we were going to the South Pacific, and that was a secret. But what were these doodads? I'd never heard them mentioned before. They turned out to be several sheets of see-through paper with spots on them. Each spot had the name of a star beside it. Each sheet was about sixteen inches across and apparently was meant to be placed in the plastic dome in the ceiling above the radio/crew chief compartment. If you picked, or found, the right sheet, it could be twisted around until the spots would line up with the stars in the heavens, if you could see them. But what did that mean? We knew what the sun and the moon looked like, but stars? We'd never heard of celestial navigation. I don't think any of us ever opened the envelopes containing that valuable aid to nighttime navigation over large bodies of water.

Between Washington and Sacramento there was quite a bit of bad weather. Not real bad, but a lot of the flight was flown on instruments. One of the places I decided to refuel was Albuquerque. They were quoting rain but no thunderstorms, broken clouds at 1,000 feet, and not much air traffic. Found the city okay and then part of the airport. I took a pass over to see which way to approach. With plenty of visibility down low through the rain, I dropped the wheels and took a left to line up on the runway for landing. As I glanced at the instruments, I saw a dark shadow out the copilot's window. "What's zat?" It was a mountain that rises out of the flat land about 3,000 or more feet and not very far from the airfield. The mountain probably wasn't as nearby as it seemed through the rain, but I still pucker some when I hear the word *Albuquerque*.

After fussing and flying formation for a few days around Sacramento, Fresno, and McClellan, the word came down to go to Hamilton Field, just north of San Francisco. "You won't know where you're going from there or when. Don't speculate. Don't talk about it. Send your mother a Western Union, but just tell her you love her. You are on security silence from right now."

Chapter 6
Flight over the Pacific

The modifications that had been made to the aircraft at the Sacramento depot were not elaborate, but a couple of them were significant. The big item was the installation of some in-cabin extra fuel supply. None of us had ever heard of it before. There wasn't any doubt now that we were expected to make some flights that were longer than a C-47 could normally fly. A C-47's normal fuel capacity was 800 gallons, with 400 gallons in each wing. Our usual consumption was about 100 gallons per hour. If we flew 150 miles per hour we could make 1,200 miles.

Somewhere, someone had been experimenting with auxiliary fuel tanks of 100-gallon capacity that were almost leakproof and snubbed to the floor. Place four of these along each side of the cabin and feed a small-bore line to our regular tanks, and all that had to be done was open a valve and the fuel would flow to the wing tanks. That made 1,600 gallons of fuel available, which meant sixteen hours of flying time. I don't recall if we had any kind of a transfer pump or if it was to be just gravity-flow. Not to worry, I guess. But just the weight of the fuel and the containers and the cradles was equal to, or more than, the allowable cargo weight according to the technical data as we had learned it. The fact that we would not have any ground echelon or supply of spare parts and equipment for an unknown period of time meant that all the gear we planned to haul along would put us seriously overweight. By then we knew our planes quite well and were confident they would handle more than the manufacturer's suggested maximum landing and takeoff weight allowable. But two or three times that weight? We didn't know how much all of our extras would weigh; still, we loaded and loaded until all the space was taken in the cabin except a narrow aisle down the middle to the cockpit. Spare engine and radio parts, replacement instruments, no smoking signs, one Thompson submachine gun, first-aid kits, a B-4 bag for each crewman's extra clothing, tool kits, C rations, and other miscellaneous bags, packages, and bundles filled the entire cabin. I took both of the two Saint Christopher medals that Aunt Adine had given me as safety insurance before I left Missoula. The crew chief found room on his shelf for the case of Ancient Age, and I hung my .45 pistol and holster on a wire over my head in the cockpit.

The other significant item added at Sacramento was a daylight navigation aid called a drift meter. When preparing a flight from point A to point B you could usually determine a compass heading or direction. But when you get in the air you are totally at the mercy of the air movement. If you held the compass heading for one hour and had a fifty mile per hour wind directly from your right, at the end of that hour you would be fifty miles to the left of your target and you'd never know it. The drift meter was like a water glass that you could use to look down through a hole (built into the floor of the plane for this purpose) and see how much you were drifting off course. Etch some lines across your glass, pick an object on the ground or a whitecap wave over water, and then twist the glass until the object below follows a line across the glass. The degree you have to turn it away from the axis of the airplane in order to follow that point below is the amount you are being blown off course by the wind. Very simple, but over a large expanse of water one of us would use the good old drift meter about every twenty minutes and our crab into the wind to compensate would be made. A great navigation tool for daytime. For nighttime, the Saint Christopher medal was called on.

At Hamilton Field a good-looking young second lieutenant gave us what little information he was privy to regarding the first

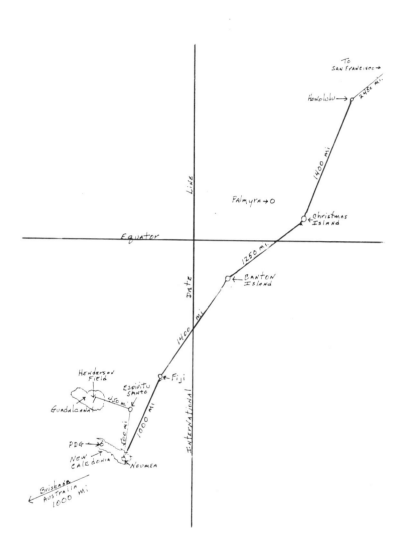

Crossing the Pacific

leg of our flight over the big Pacific Ocean. It didn't seem like adequate information, but we were too dumb to ask any intelligent questions. He did give us this information and these instructions:

"You will be landing at Hickam Field, which is just across the bay from Honolulu, if you find it. Hickam tower frequency is such and such. Go around Diamond Head and up Waikiki Beach a mile or so. Hickam will be off your left at about ten or eleven o'clock, across the bay. The distance from Hamilton to Hickam is right at 2,400 miles.

"You will be flying individually, not as a formation. Takeoff will be at twenty- to thirty-minute intervals. You will each be assigned an altitude at which to fly and each will have different power settings so we can determine which is the most efficient. If you get there give us a call and we'll know your settings were okay. Hey, that's a joke. Don't look so pale.

"The Coast Guard reports no serious weather conditions, but they don't know beyond 500 miles. There is a radio beam out of Hilo that you might be able to receive an hour or so before you reach the island of Oahu.

"Maintain radio silence.

"Here is a list of power settings for each plane and an approximate takeoff time. It will be dark for takeoff, but you will gain *x* number of hours of daylight, so you'll have plenty of light left for landing at Hickam. Hickam will brief you on the balance of your flight to Australia.

"Incidentally, the magnetic compass heading to Hickam is such and such, but remember the direction will change some as you go along."

So this was it. I guess we were about to make a little history. Naturally we had to feel excitement, but I recall being calm, confident, relaxed, and ready, not cocky or macho. New adventures were almost a daily occurrence, so why not feel at ease about this one? Here we were heading out on an unknown mission to a faraway part of the world that we barely knew existed, over a body of water so large we couldn't imagine it. I guess we had to be adaptable. I don't recall ever having any written orders sending me away. We didn't have any automatic pilot. No navigator. Probably no sense or we wouldn't be doing this, but we adapted. There was evidently a list of crews for the thirteen airplanes, which I first saw in 1988, forty-six years later. These thirteen planes and crews were each a story by themselves, though the memory does get foggy as to specifics.

This I clearly remember: the way it felt to taxi that C-47 out toward the end of a big, long runway and knowing that it would be a long, long flight over a lot of water before the landing gear touched back down on Mother Earth. I feel it now but can't describe it. So what! There was work to be done.

We didn't have preflight written checklists in those days, but my hand touched every control or gauge that had to be working properly, to be sure all was in order. Because of the extreme overweight, I wanted as much runway as possible so I got as far as possible to the starting end. I think the tail wheel must have hung off the runway. After a final check and a good listen to the sweet-sounding engines, I released the brakes and pushed the throttles just a little more than maximum forward. The roll began. I could feel the overload, but the roll accelerated very nicely. The speed indicator rose just like during any other takeoff, and lo and behold, by the time we were halfway down the runway, the speed was over normal takeoff. I pulled the tail down a little, the wheels gently left the ground, and we gained some altitude. That plane, with that wing and with those engines, was so good that it didn't even know it was being abused. It just purred along over the bay, over the lights of San Francisco, and over the Golden Gate on the way to the other side of the Pacific Ocean.

My assigned altitude was 8,000 feet, so in my naïveté I thought that meant 8,000 feet. There were some clouds and some thunder-heads that could have been avoided by going left or right a few miles or up or down some, but that nice young second lieutenant said 8,000 feet, so that's what we maintained.

My assigned power settings, both boost and RPMs, were about as low as you could use and still stay in the air; but again, that's what the man said and that's what he got. Had I known enough to go up to 9,000 feet and then gradually descend to 8,000 feet, we could have picked up a few miles per hour air speed and maintained that for a long time. Nothing said this maneuver couldn't be done several times on a single flight, but that we didn't know. A day or two later, as we became veterans at this, we learned that and many other fine points of properly handling a flying machine.

We didn't see any other airplane, hear any radio chatter, or even see any ships afloat. That is, except when Shea came in with, "Hey, look down below. That's a battleship." I knew his voice very well, but he must have been some distance away, because we didn't see anything. And it wasn't a battleship, probably a destroyer. Our battleships were all in the far Pacific or sunk in Pearl Harbor.

The first time we had any idea of about where on the line to Hickam we really were was when we intersected the beam from Hilo. Our radio operator, Ben King, had picked up Hilo's A-quadrant signal some time back, but that didn't tell us much. In Morse code the A-quadrant is a dot-dash, dot-dash. On these old-fashioned radio ranges they could direct those quadrants covering one-quarter of a circle outward from the range station. The N-quadrant is a dash-dot, dash-dot. By slightly overlapping those two signals the sound would be a steady sound; hence it was referred to as the beam. That would give us a position on a line out from Hilo but it didn't say whether you were too close to the big island of Hawaii or too close to Alaska or right on your planned route to Hickam. At least it was comforting because we knew that we were about three-quarters of the way there. Not long after that, three fighter planes from Hickam came out to look us over. That should have been their procedure a few months earlier: December 7, 1941, to be exact.

The atmosphere in the cockpit changed considerably. It wasn't so lonely anymore. Ben King didn't usually talk much, but he started talking, obviously relieved. Thompson, the crew chief, wasn't much for talk either, but he started talking, obviously relieved. Bryce Smith, the copilot, seldom talked, but he started talking, obviously relieved. The pilot joined in the babble. He was also relieved. He had just taken his first leak since San Francisco. Through the relief tube. Right into the Pacific Ocean. That was real relief.

After an elapsed time of fifteen hours and forty-five minutes we finally touched down at Hickam Field. We had fifteen minutes of fuel left over. Today the FAA would frown at that small amount of margin as being inadequate. But that fifteen minutes of fuel was okay by me.

Somewhere along the line, four of the eight extra fuel tanks in the cabin were removed. It was probably done at Hickam. I don't recall any more flights of over nine or ten hours.

Hickam to Christmas Island

I had never heard of Christmas Island when somebody said, "That's where you are headed on the next leg of your journey." Christmas Island was apparently located southwest of Hawaii. As small as it was, there was no point in giving us a map of the island, because if you can find the island you can see the strip, since they are almost the same size. The somebody gave us the longitude, the latitude, and the nautical miles as well as the magnetic heading. We logged nine hours on that leg; thus I presume it was about 1,500 miles from Hickam. Simple to get there, I guess. Just head out in the proper direction, fly nine hours, and if you see an island, land on it. There aren't any other islands for many miles, so you don't get any alternative. The drift meter got plenty of use that day. The main worry was wind direction. That included all directions: front, back, left, and right, because it would move us off the intended track. In this area there was no information about current weather conditions. Old mariners' maps didn't record anything about prevailing winds, and the ocean currents data didn't help us much.

The Rickenbacker Incident

Capt. Eddie Rickenbacker was heading over to the southwest Pacific on official War Department business. (He should have hitched a ride with one of us.) He had a B-17, a four-engine bomber, with a crew of eight or ten military. One crewman was a full-fledged navigator who, so the story goes, stumbled while boarding their plane at Hickam and dropped his sextant on the concrete. He picked it up and climbed aboard. Capt. Bill Cherry, the pilot, the rest of his crew, Rickenbacker, and his aide climbed in, and they took off for Palmyra Island, which would be some 200 or 300 miles west and north of our destination that day, Christmas Island. They didn't navigate by drift meter and luck. They had a trained navigator using an expensive sextant that could read the stars, the moon, and the sun. By having an accurate twenty-four-hour watch set on Greenwich time, charts, azimuths, horizons, and a compass, and perhaps even having been a Nobel candidate in math, theoretically the navigator could place the B-17 accurately over any spot on earth at that particular moment. But something didn't work. They were lost out over that ocean that day. I don't laugh. It wasn't funny, but it was so incongruous that equipped as they were, they were lost. I didn't think we were lost, yet, but we still had some miles to go to our planned destination with only a drift meter to keep us going in the proper direction.

Our radio operator, Ben, had picked up a plain English radio transmission on one of his available frequencies, but not on the universal emergency frequency, 550. It went something like this: "To anyone receiving this message. This is U.S. Army B-17 # ———

heading for Palmyra. We have exceeded our ETA [estimated time of arrival] and have begun circular search procedure. [That means starting in small circles and gradually increasing radius.] We have less than four hours of fuel." The signal came in quite strong, but over water this did not necessarily mean it was real close. We had a radio direction finder that had been installed at Sacramento, but it only pointed toward the transmission on 550. And it would only receive for forty or fifty miles. But for some reason the B-17 never did transmit on the 550 wavelength. We heard a later transmission with information that they had less than two hours of fuel and that the VIP on board was Rickenbacker.

By then we had used up some of our time and a lot of our fuel zigzagging back and forth and shooting off in various directions every time we saw some imaginary object in the sky or on the water. Some others of our squadron were doing the same type search, but even though we could communicate with them, we couldn't tell our relative locations, because we were just scattered somewhere over that big patch of water. Some of our planes searched an extra day or two out of Christmas Island, some did the same out of Canton Island, and some went on to Fiji. As I recall, it was by pilot option what we chose to do. Our plane searched until dark one day, all of the following day, and two or three hours at first light the next day out of Canton Island.

Rickenbacker and a couple of members of that B-17 crew were rescued three weeks after ditching in the ocean.

Near the end of hostilities I was at Bergstrom Air Force Base in Texas when Captain Cherry, the pilot of Rickenbacker's B-17 and one of the very few survivors of three weeks in their life raft, came by. I think he was a colonel by then. We talked at length about the situations that could have conceivably contributed to his being unable to hit Palmyra back then. He was quite sure, as was the investigating team, that some damage had been done to the navigator's sextant when he dropped it at Hickam, so that he was taking incorrect position shots. That, of course, resulted in his track being to either the left or the right of the intended heading. Cherry didn't have any idea where they went into the water or which direction it was from Palmyra. They know now where they were finally found but had no idea from which direction they had come. If memory serves me, he also said that during those twenty or thirty days they were in the water they saw not one vessel or aircraft. They should have had a drift meter. I rubbed it in!

During the early 1960s, when I lived in Scottsdale, Captain Rickenbacker, then president of Eastern Airlines, came to Phoenix to promote his airline. At a press lunch reception for him I was asked by the chairman to sit at Rickenbacker's table. Captain Rickenbacker had always made it known that he wanted to shake the hand of anyone who had worked on his rescue. Well, we didn't rescue him, but we tried hard and sure risked our own lives; thus I always thought we qualified for that handshake. After some chamber-of-commerce-type remarks about Phoenix and about Eastern Airlines, the chairman said, "Captain Rickenbacker, everyone knows about your terrible accident in the Pacific Ocean way back in 1942. Several planes and many naval vessels searched for survivors, but after a few days they abandoned the search and gave you and your crew up for dead. Everyone knows that two or three of you survived, under extremely adverse conditions. The story of you catching a lone sea gull that landed on your head and helped you to survive is a classic. We also know that you publicly stated on numerous occasions that you wanted to shake the hand of every person who had searched for you. We are pleased to introduce you to one of the military pilots who spent time doing just that in that big Pacific Ocean, almost twenty years ago. Meet George Wamsley."

Rickenbacker was a crotchety old guy and getting mighty old by that time. Tough, too. He looked me straight in the eye, no trace of a smile. "You looked in the wrong place!" he practically shouted. There wasn't a sound. My heart sank to my shoes. My face turned red in embarrassment. Then he put on a big grin, shook my hand, patted me on the back, and said, "Thanks, buddy."

Christmas Island to Canton

When we finally got our plane fueled and put to bed that evening at Christmas Island, a young GI stationed there with a few fellow Yanks came by. He said, "I'll give you a hundred bucks for a quart of whiskey."

"Tell you what I'll do. You guard the airplane tonight, and if it's okay at first light tomorrow I'll *give* you a quart of whiskey," I replied.

He thought that was a real good deal, so we shook on it. This deal gave the four of us a chance to sleep on cots. When a beautiful South Sea island morning greeted us, we found our plane was secure. The quart of Ancient Age was sacrificed to a happy GI.

Christmas was a beautiful tropical island from the air. There were very few soldiers around and no natives. There were waving palm trees and a shoreline with a picture perfect half-moon bay, probably a mile across, with white sand beaches and dark blue ocean water. Just like the travel pictures.

Canton was a six- or seven-hour flight, but our early start and plenty of fuel gave us a chance to search a much wider swath than just a straight line. By now we knew that the pilot of the missing aircraft was Bill Cherry. and that Rickenbacker was on board. We also knew that they must have crashed into the ocean, because the last anyone had heard was that they only had one hour of fuel remaining. We flew about 1,000 feet above water and swiveled our heads constantly. Any time one of us saw something afloat we'd swing over for a closer look. Most times our sightings were imagination or tricks from the light. But we did see a few objects, such as a palm tree, a discarded packing crate that could have come from anywhere, a wake made by a couple of dolphins, and more gallons of water than anyone could imagine. We crossed the equator on this leg but didn't have any time for the traditional celebration with Davy Jones. We didn't find any sign of the B-17. We found Canton

Island, but I remember nothing about being there. Must have been tired.

I am reasonably sure that our crew and old #634 spent a full day working out of Canton in continuation of the Rickenbacker search, but the details are long forgotten. Flight records, like my Form 5, were reconstructed from miscellaneous guess notes from somebody, not me, and maybe even some notes made by the crew chief, from time to time. The flight conditions we experienced were not conducive to record keeping. Numerous trips, journeys, and missions were never recorded at all. Record keeping just wasn't a high priority at this time.

On to Fiji

We proceeded southwesterly toward the supergreen country of Fiji. It was a nine-hour flight, and after these past several days of tropical heat in dirty, wrinkled clothes and with the anticipation of a good swim followed by good food and sleeping accommodations, we were in high spirits. When we located the tower frequency, we asked for landing instructions. The tower called back: "Army 634, what is the color of the day?" I'd never heard of any color of any day; I just wanted to land. "No color of the day known," was our feeble response. "What is the word of the day, Army 634?" I'd never heard of anything like that either. I thought maybe they would send us away. After all, security is security. But since they already had several of our squadron on the ground, the password procedure was waived.

Fiji to New Caledonia

The next leg of the journey was to the French colony of New Caledonia. That country is an island 200 miles long and maybe 20 miles wide. The capital is Nouméa, a town about the size of Ronan, located on the southern portion of the island. On the side nearest Australia, up near the northern tip of the island, is another small town about the size of Charlo. I don't recall ever seeing Plaines des Gaiacs (PDG) clearly, as every time I was nearby it rained and I was busy searching for the airfield. Some of our planes had left Fiji the previous day for this small town, where there was fuel and accommodations. PDG would be our last island stop before arriving in Australia. We didn't have maps telling us anything about the island but didn't anticipate any problem finding PDG either.

The naval battle of the Coral Sea had just finished in a victory for the U.S. fleet. Their first win, I believe. The Coral Sea touches the north portion of New Caledonia (at PDG) and extends north to the Solomons and west to New Guinea and Australia.

Just before we were going to take off from Fiji, two navy officers in fine uniforms came out of Operations and said, "Hear you're going to New Cal. How about hitching a ride?"

"No problem. Get your gear and hop on," I said.

So they did. About an hour out, I invited them up front. One sat in the copilot's seat, and the other squatted between us. I showed them some instruments and told them about where we had been to get this far and also that in about five more hours we'd be in PDG. "PDG! We have to get to Nouméa. We have to report aboard ship there. Maybe you could drop us off at Nouméa." There wasn't anything in my orders that stated that I had to go by PDG. I was headed for Brisbane from anywhere.

New Caledonia was about 200 miles long, and since we were heading almost perpendicular to the length of the island, we would just head for the shore and go up overland until we got to the other side, and then it shouldn't be hard to locate Nouméa. We ran into some heavy rain about thirty minutes out and presumed it would rain over the land and also on the other side. One of the navy officers volunteered that on this side of New Cal, all along the south half, there was a very visible reef about five miles offshore that ran down to the south tip of the island. We had neither weather information nor any communication with the other side of the island. This lack of information would make it hard to know when to go down so that we could proceed visually.

We went down to about 100 feet and watched for the reef. Sure enough, there it was. When we could see land through the rain, we turned left (port, the navy guy said) and went around the end of New Cal with no problem. We started up the western side looking for something that looked like a harbor or an airstrip or even a town like Nouméa. A few miles later, out aways from the shore we were following and absolutely dead ahead, was the biggest piece of floating machinery I'd ever seen. It was an aircraft carrier. Signal lights, must have been more than one, were flashing right at us. I presumed they were asking for identification, but I still didn't know any color of the day or word of the day or how to read fast Morse code. Besides, there wasn't any time. I used the landing light and had time enough to send "Okay, okay," or a portion thereof. By that time we were going right by the carrier at about their deck level, and I swear I saw about a hundred antiaircraft guns following us every inch of the way. None of them fired. Maybe we didn't look like much of a threat, but maybe the gunnery officer knew what a C-47 looked like, too.

The shoreline was about a half-mile away, and sitting right there on the airstrip were a bunch of Grumman F-4 aircraft. We learned later that the carrier had taken a hit on the flight deck during the battle of the Coral Sea and was undergoing some temporary repairs, so the carrier pilots had parked their planes on the Nouméa airstrip. We figured it would take us about an hour to fly up to PDG, where we would meet the rest of our planes that had flown in from Fiji. The ones that had left Fiji the day before would probably have gone on to Brisbane today. And they had. Records, such as they are, indicate that seven planes had departed from PDG, and from the memories of most of the crews, while no two people recall the exact numbers today (1990), we sorta agree that seven planes and seven crews did not depart from PDG. Instead, they were stolen, ex-propriated, or commandeered by that other branch of the service, the navy, and that by the man himself, Bull Halsey. He had immediate use for us. He grounded the six planes from our squadron that were at PDG.

My Form 5 records show I stayed overnight with those navy guys at Nouméa (code name: Tontouta) and then went up and joined our guys in the mud of PDG the following day, October 25, 1942.

Chapter 7
Guadalcanal

PDG, Plaines des Gaiacs, this stopover was located on the extreme north end of New Caledonia. The name is probably French, and the spelling and pronunciation were difficult to translate into English. However, all we had to remember was that the code name was PDG.

The runways were wet, sticky, slippery red mud most of the time. Army engineers were trying to build a quality runway while keeping the strip open for transient aircraft coming and going to and from who knew where. There was only a makeshift tower, with very few taxiways and minimal accommodations for planes and crews. And very little military coordination.

Part of the problem, in retrospect, was that the war was not going too well for our side and was not very far away. The Japanese had significant forces in the Solomons to the north and New Guinea to the northwest and major facilities in New Britain, while our good old navy was not yet recovered from Pearl Harbor. Besides, from a political standpoint this war in the Pacific was still a second-rate war. Congress and the military were still committed to the European theater of operations. We, the Thirty-third Troop Carrier Squadron of thirteen planes and fifty-two people, were getting into the center of a complex situation. Navy, army, marines, Air Corps, French, island natives, British, Japanese, Japanese navy, Japanese air force. Egad, and we weren't yet a week out of California.

At this time, the seven Thirty-third Squadron crews at PDG were:

1. Cartwright, Ridley, Grabner, Borchert
2. Schnieders, George and Franni, Dorland, Anderson
3. Hensman, Dillman, Kirsch, Lamar
4. Carlson, Holden, Bloodsworth, Kavelesky
5. Glotzbach, Schwensen, Zorbach, Bradley
6. Wamsley, Smith, Thompson, King
7. Names not available

Six of our planes had scooted out of PDG early enough so that Halsey's commandeering message didn't catch them. Thus we were now seven crews without a commanding officer, with no ground echelon and no idea of what we were supposed to do. However, it was clear that we weren't at liberty to beat it on to Brisbane. We were to sit tight at PDG, in the rain and red mud, and wait for something to happen, good or bad. We were fed by some kind of a base facility, by furnishing our own mess kit, or by the engineers, who were also building roads, buildings, and an airport. We were bogged down there for nearly a week. We had no communication with our other planes, which had reached Brisbane and were sent immediately on to Port Moresby, New Guinea.

The only good thing I can recall happening at PDG took place on a miserable, rainy evening in our warehouse—pardon me, our tin barracks. We had plenty much mud on the floor, some army cots, a few benches, and a couple of tables. The three sixty-watt lamps hanging from the ceiling barely shone through the dust. Somebody was playing cards. The tin door opened. The wind and rain blew in, and about eight well-dressed, high-ranking navy officers accompanied by two news bureau correspondents stepped inside. Not very far in, though. This didn't look like a very good spot for them to spend the night. They fidgeted, talked in low tones, and didn't move much. Perhaps they were expecting a Holiday Inn. After a few minutes of this, Schwensen's voice boomed out from the card game, "Hey, any you guys less than a second lieutenant close the door!" That broke everyone up. They came farther in, down to where we were lounging. One of the correspondents said, "Say, aren't you Franni Schnieders from Loyola? I'm Bill Henry, sports columnist from the *LA Times*. And that's your brother, George Schnieders. Who are these other guys?" Everybody relaxed, told stories, and visited for a long time. Bill Henry wrote a great front-page column about this incident. He gathered we'd win the war some way.

This might be a good time to clarify the scenario: Before we got anywhere near PDG, the marines, who had landed on Guadalcanal a few weeks earlier, were having one helluva time. The navy that put them there was hard put to resupply them with a fraction of the equipment that the marines needed. The Japanese controlled all of Guadalcanal except Henderson Field (airstrip), and some days they controlled that. Our navy had lost many vessels to a vastly superior Japanese navy force but didn't even think of pulling back. Our forces outscored the Japanese but were running out of firepower. (You heard about Iron Bottom Bay that was at Guadalcanal.)

The luxury liner *President Coolidge* had been pressed into military service and was bringing a load of supplies, ammunition, equipment, and a complete hospital to Espíritu Santo in the New Hebrides, about 450 miles from PDG. The *President Coolidge* pulled into the friendly harbor of Espíritu Santo on October 26, 1942. Unfortunately, as the ship entered the harbor, it hit two U.S. mines and began to sink (Ira Wolfert, eyewitness). Surprisingly, only 5 lives were lost, because of the proximity to shore. The vessel sank rapidly and actually rolled over as it went down into the coral reefs. Salvage effort, for the cargo, that is, began immediately. I don't know just what percentage of the cargo was retrieved, but there were piles of equipment, crates and boxes scattered for two or three hundred yards along the shoreline. Only 5 lives were lost; 5,435 were saved ("Wreck of the *Coolidge*" by David Doubilet. *National Geographic*, April 1988). The *Coolidge* sank on the second day we were at PDG, but we didn't know about it until four or five days later when we were dispatched to Espíritu Santo.

Because of these existing conditions, Admiral Halsey, being brand-new on the job, thought maybe, just maybe, our C-47s could ferry some of the most critical items from Espíritu Santo to Guadalcanal by air. The navy had no air transport, and their water transport was cut to ribbons. Halsey's title was Commander, South Pacific, and that included all branches of the military. He had been in command for probably ten days now. (MacArthur was Commander, Southwest Pacific, and the command boundary passed between New Caledonia and Australia.)

U.S. Navy and Marine fighter planes were doing extremely well, victorywise. But Admiral Halsey was in Nouméa, quite nervous. General Vandegrift, Marines, was on Guadalcanal and very nervous. Both commanders were vitally concerned with the lack of transport and supplies: the Thirty-third had six planes in Brisbane and seven planes in PDG.

Regardless of bad weather we went back and forth the estimated 200 miles from PDG to Tontouta (Nouméa) for two days, hauling supplies needed by the new temporary theater command headquarters at Nouméa. Then the next day we all were to go to Espíritu Santo, three or three and a half hours away. It was time for the mandatory 100-hour check on our airplanes, so we did it after dark. Since we had no mechanics or ground crew, we just did it ourselves: pilot, copilot, crew chief, radioman, using the book of instructions in the "glove compartment." One item that was to be checked, along with many, many others, was the trim tab. That was done by turning the trim tab control, located by the pilot's right knee, to one extreme position, very dangerous, then getting out of the aircraft and by flashlight visually checking that the trim unit actually had moved completely into the maximum position. Then whoever was doing that had to climb back into the cockpit and turn the tab control to the opposite extreme position and then climb back out and by flashlight verify that the trim unit had gone into the opposite position from the previous check. All was well. This was sort of like doing a lube job for your car, changing the engine oil, and getting your car checked over for a long trip. We fueled up and were ready to go bright and early the next morning.

We had not heard of a pretakeoff written checklist, whereby one pilot in the cockpit calls out the item to be checked and the other looks at that item, touches it, and verifies it by saying, "Check." What we did in those days was just a cursory look-see. If the important things like fuel, RPM, oil pressure, flaps, and alternator looked okay, we'd presume we were prepared for takeoff. We didn't bother to notice that one trim tab control was in extreme left position.

With throttle, boost, and RPM pushed forward, the plane started down the narrow runway. The aircraft seemed to pull left a little, so I pushed in some more left engine throttle. As we gained speed, the plane seemed to still pull left, so I braked the right gear some and pulled right throttle back a little. We had no cargo, so the acceleration was quite rapid. I rolled in a little right rudder and that seemed to help, so I rolled in some more. It helped some more, but by now we were getting quite close to the left side of the runway and going pretty fast, too. As we approached flying speed the plane was almost hopping. Just off the left of the runway was a construction trench about six feet deep and beyond that some torpedo bombers.

I hollered to Smitty, "Help with right rudder!" He thought I didn't mean it, that it was just a turbulent takeoff. I rolled in some more right rudder trim and gave more left engine throttle and more right aileron as the plane became airborne just over the trench and was fast approaching the parked torpedo bombers. One more turn on the right rudder trim tab and everything began to smooth out, except it wasn't certain we would clear the bombers. I was prepared to say, "Oh, shit!," which is the standard pilot report just before he goes in. We cleared the first bomber by the grace of God, with inches to spare. However, our plane was flying and we were gaining altitude. I looked down at the trim tab and it was exactly on zero, where it should have been before takeoff. Obviously, one of us had failed to return the tab to zero position last night during the 100-hour check. That was as close to a deadly accident without having one as I can imagine.

Not much was said in the cabin for about the first hour out over water. Finally, Smitty said, "George, do you still have those two Saint Christopher medals?" I thought he wanted one. That he had seen the light. That he was convinced they worked. Then he added, "I think you'd better get out the other one. The one in your pocket must be worn out!"

Guadalcanal! Just the spoken word would conjure up visions of disaster. We actually knew very little about the place, but during the past few days rumors had become fact that the entire action was taking a turn for the worse. The marines had an almost impossible job of holding the portion of the island that they had taken at great cost. The opposing navies seemed to be moving for a decisive kill, which could go either way. The ground reinforcements had been aboard the *Coolidge* and were now ashore at Espíritu Santo, but there was no way to get all of them and their equipment to Guadalcanal because of the major sea battles going on just offshore. Seven C-47s that could haul only half-loads weren't going to make more difference than a drop in the bucket, but we were gung ho to do whatever might help. We headed out for Espíritu Santo to do something. The code name for Espíritu Santo was Buttons.

It was three and a half hours over water to Buttons. The navy guys at the airfield sure didn't know what to do with us. They knew we were available to haul whatever we could pile aboard from the merchandise on the beach, but no one was really in charge to make decisions and give orders. Their shore hands were few in number and worn out from round-the-clock emergency duty. At least Buttons had fuel.

I asked one of the navy officers, "How do we find Henderson Field?"

"Oh, you head out about this direction," he said as he indicated a somewhat northwesterly direction with his hand. "About 150 miles out you will see San Cristobal. Stay along the north side of that island. When you run out of island hold your heading for about 150 miles till you hit the tip of Guadalcanal. Stay on the north side for about 200 miles, and you will see Henderson Field (code: Cactus) cut out of the palm trees. They don't have much of a radio tower at the field, but call them on frequency xxx. Be sure to ask them for the condition of the field, because sometimes they don't own it. When they give you the condition of the field, if it's green, it's controlled by marines and you can land. If it's yellow, they are sharing with Japs or maybe soon will be. They may suggest something, but you will have to be the judge of what to do next. There is no alternative airfield except back here. You will have to get there before dark. Good luck." He didn't mention accommodations.

"What if the condition is red?" I asked.

"Guess you'll have to come back here. We don't have many lights, but if it's stormy we'll turn on an antiaircraft searchlight. Those lights can penetrate 20,000 feet through clouds." I didn't think that bit through very well.

Henderson had no fuel. Let's see. Four hours or more up there, an hour or so hanging around wondering what to do. Then four or more hours back here to begin looking for that searchlight beam. Thanks to the confusion, there wasn't time to worry!

We did not fly in formation on the way from PDG to Buttons. We got strung out on purpose, because we were 100 percent vulnerable to enemy fighter planes that might be in the same area. Guess the thought was it was better to lose one plane than six or seven. But we didn't spend much time fretting about that. At Buttons it took some time to get a plane loaded, pointed toward Cactus, fueled, and off the ground. Thus we got strung out more. Besides, I'm sure the marines at Cactus didn't want more than one or two strange planes on their runway at the same time. That's in case we made it that far.

By the time we were loaded and ready to go it was evident there would only be about one hour of daylight left when we reached Cactus. A fellow came and asked to hitch a ride. He had a khaki uniform with a correspondent insignia, hence was a legitimate passenger, fool that he might be. He turned out to be Ira Wolfert, who during the past week had spent time on the ground at Guadalcanal and three or four days aboard a navy vessel and had watched the *Coolidge* go down and now wanted to go back and see who was winning the battle for the Solomons. In addition to dispatches to his paper, he was preparing a book called *Battle for the Solomons*, which would become a good seller when published in 1943. In that book he referred to me as a rosy-cheeked second lieutenant. Actually, I was a grizzled, unkempt veteran of one week in the combat zone.

This first trip into Cactus was a memorable event for me. The weather was perfect for flying and clear enough that we found San Cristobal after an hour or so. We proceeded up the northern shoreline until we ran out of island to follow. We moved on over water, nudging left just a little, which was expected to give us sight of Guadalcanal after about an hour. Sure enough, just like the man said, there it was. We went up along the shoreline, about a half-mile out over the water and probably 1,000 feet above. We started looking for Henderson Field right away, even though we were told it would be about 200 miles farther on.

Our anxiety grew, and we moved in a bit closer to shore. As we neared the shore, some strange red lights seemed to be coming up toward us at intervals of about a second or two. Some of those red lights came closer, and some even went on by in front of us and overhead. Then we realized that we were being machine-gunned. Every fifth bullet was a tracer so the mean guy firing the gun could better tell where he was shooting. This gave him an idea of how much to compensate in order to hit his target. We were evidently the target. I headed out into the ocean, away from shore, right then! But I didn't know how far those guns could reach. Just to be sure,

I added about two extra miles, which put us out about four or five miles. But our eyesight got better, too. If Henderson Field was along that shore and if it belonged to our marines, we'd sure as heck find it.

Before our ETA was up, I decided to talk to Cactus Tower. By now I really wanted to know if we had friends down there. On the suggested frequency in a clear, calm (with maybe a little swagger) voice I called in, "Cactus Tower, this is Army 634. Over." Deadly quiet. Silence. Maybe a little louder and more demanding style would help. "Cactus Tower, this is Army 634. Come in." Nothing. I'd wait a bit.

Then, "Cactus Tower to unknown ship. Wait," came over our speaker.

I wasn't too interested in waiting; therefore, I soon came back, "Cactus Tower. This is Army 634. What is the condition of your field?" But by this time my voice was much less macho and about one octave higher.

Still no response. Finally he came back with, "This is Cactus Tower to unknown ship . . . wait."

Now we had spotted the airstrip. It was not far in from the shore, but no planes were visible in the air or on the ground. I have no idea how high-pitched my voice was, but it was probably a squeal when I called out, "This is Army 634! We must know the condition of your field!" Nothing. We'd made a couple of circles out over the water, and time was marching on. I could see just a little action down on the strip, a few jeeps and trucks, and by now I could pick out some F-4 planes backed in under the trees, but they didn't seem to be coming out to shoot us down. All seemed quiet. No hand-to-hand battles on the strip, no bombs bursting in air, no machine-gun tracers. So one last try. "Cactus Tower. This is Army 634, preparing to land." I thought that was pretty good, but it evidently didn't impress Cactus Tower. No response.

The wind normally comes in from the water, which meant that we would want to touch down at the far end of the field and roll to a stop at the end closest to the water. I started a conventional landing approach as taught in flight school: go downwind about two miles parallel to the strip, throttle back some, lower the gear, pass the end of the strip about a mile, slow down some more, go on base leg, turn on approach leg, lower more flaps, and prepare to land. About this time the plane is supposed to be almost two miles from the point of touchdown, but in this case that seemed to be much too far out. We were flying over manned machine-gun emplacements that were pointed at the field. They appeared to turn around and point at us, but no one fired. After landing and rolling to a stop and snuggling up to the trees, we were greeted by a big he-man husky marine. I asked him, "Hey, who's in those foxholes up there?"

"That line of them close to the field are ours, and those about a mile back are theirs." That was the inspiration for a new technique not taught in flight school. It's called the gear down and spin in approach. We used it regularly thereafter when we didn't know which end of the strip our guys owned or whose troops were close by. In this approach, go over the strip perpendicularly at 100 feet or less, look both ways up and down the strip to see where our guys are, drop the gear as you make a short turn, don't gain much or any altitude, crank the turn tight, have the gear locked, come out of your turn at the same time as you are lined up with the runway, and be ready to touch down. Then finish your roll as you reach the end of the strip where our guys are.

It was getting dark by now, and heading back to Buttons, about four and a half hours away, to a strip with only a searchlight, just didn't seem the proper way to go. The marines had unloaded our goodies in a hurry and spirited them off into the jungle. Warned that we should be mindful of unannounced high-level or low-level bombs or bullets from some fanatical Japanese pilot, we put our C-47 as much into the trees as we could, and that was not much. A friendly-type marine led us down a path through the woods about 100 yards off the strip to a lone tent that had about ten folding canvas cots. Just outside the flap was a slit trench that would hold about ten guys. He warned us about no lights, no matches, and no walking around. "Snipers show up frequently somewhere within our perimeter, which, incidentally, is about two square miles, but mainly they are for harassment and testing our defenses. Don't fire that pistol," he informed us.

He forgot a couple of things. He didn't feed us and he forgot to say, "Have a nice sleep," before he went somewhere in the dark. We couldn't locate any boards to hold the canvas in place on the heads and feet of the cots. It was not at all comfortable. But the atmosphere wasn't conducive to sleep anyway. And to top it off, a slow-flying aircraft came cruising over in the middle of the night. We weren't asleep anyway, but we sure thought we should get in that slit trench. But we didn't want to be the first ones to hit the dirt, and we couldn't hear anyone moving around. There wasn't anyone passing the word to take cover, no air-raid siren. We held our ground inside the tent, but we didn't like it. The plane went back and forth over the field for some time, like an hour, but no bombs were dropped and no shots were fired from the ground. This was our introduction to Washing-Machine Charlie. Charlie was a devious plan by the Japanese to disrupt our guys on the ground. It didn't seem to bother the marines. We found out the Japanese did the harassing bit almost every night. Once in a while Charlie would drop a small bomb, but most nights he would just go home after an hour or two overhead. When nighttime naval battles were taking place, sometimes as close as four or five miles from the strip, Charlie would not show up. That was my only night to RON (remain over night) on Guadalcanal.

When we got back to Buttons the following morning, we found we had lost our first plane. Fortunately, all of the crew survived. Carlson was the pilot. He didn't get loaded early enough to get to Guadalcanal before dark, and of course you can't and don't land at Henderson at night. He decided on an early morning takeoff, like about 3:00 A.M., in order to reach Cactus by first light and get back to Buttons to fuel and back to Tontouta before day came again.

Buttons had minimal runway lights, but if started in the right direction the plane should be able to get off. Carlson's plane carried about 5,000 pounds of hand grenades, which the navy guys had taken off the *Coolidge.*

Carlson started down the runway. He couldn't see much, especially not the two trucks using the runway as a road as they hauled supplies back and forth. Carlson was almost up to flying speed when his wing clipped one of the trucks. This wheeled him around almost sideways and into the second truck. It also set the plane on fire. Before the plane came to a stop, it went broadside into a B-17 parked off the runway. Carlson, in a great burst of speed, went back into the cabin to help the guys there to get out through the cargo door. Since the flames were still all outside the plane, the hand grenades were not exploding, but there was lots of fire outside. The guys in back jumped out the cargo door with Carlson right behind them. As he was going through the door, he noticed a deflated emergency raft beside the door. For some reason, he decided it was about the only thing he could save, so he grabbed the raft, which was almost as large as he was, and leaped out the door and away from the flames. He was glad nobody took a picture. As Carlson was exiting the cockpit, copilot Holden had reached up overhead and opened the escape hatch and "got the hell outa there," to quote him.

There was a real mess. One truck driver was killed, and two aircraft were totaled. We lost one of our squadron planes, but all our crew members were safe and, of course, Carlson had bravely rescued the inflatable raft.

Many years later Carlson was having a cup of coffee with another bird colonel that he had just met. They mentioned their overseas areas, and the colonel said that he would have been involved in a special flight into Guadalcanal in his B-17 in 1942 "if some goddamn fool C-47 pilot hadn't run into my parked plane at Espíritu Santo and burned it up." Carlson said, "I really hate to tell you this, but I was the pilot of that C-47."

November 1942 was a busy flying time, according to my Form 5 flying record. Back and forth between the islands of New Hebrides and the Solomons, mostly over water. The work was totally exhausting; I remember that part. But it couldn't have been any worse than what those guys on the ground were experiencing. The only days my Form 5 doesn't show some time logged are the tenth and seventeenth. Maybe they were Sundays.

On November 8 the navy guys at Buttons said things were pretty tight at Cactus, but we should take a load anyway. They said Cactus wouldn't let us stay overnight, as they didn't want any planes on the strip. The navy guys also promised to have the searchlight on and to have a few vehicles with lights along the sides of the runway back here, at Buttons, in case we returned during the night.

Hensman took off about an hour ahead of me. We would both be returning to Buttons about midnight, we thought. The formalities of landing at Cactus had been modified some. The marines had cleared out most of the Japanese between the strip and the water, but not all. There was no conversation with the ground. If there was heavy activity in the immediate area they would call us as soon as they saw us and tell us to beat it. Meaning, go away.

When we got there, we made a straight-in approach from the water and touched down on the very first part of the strip, the marines waved us to come to one end, and that we did. Hensman had been there, unloaded, and taken off toward the water. He was shot down by ground fire about the time he reached the shoreline and crashed into the water. I remember it as being only a mile or maybe two miles from shore at most. There were no survivors. We lost four good people: S. Sgt. Pilot Ray Hensman, S. Sgt. Pilot Robert Dillman, T. Sgt. Albert Kirsch, and Corp. Jim Laniar.

By the time we were unloaded, it was almost getting dark. One of the marines on the unloading detail told me Hensman had made a gradual right turn just after takeoff and suggested I not make a right turn until after we got over the water. I did him one better.

After a maximum climb takeoff, I edged off toward the left and got as high as I could as fast as I could. We saw no indication we were being shot at, so after a few minutes we headed into heavy rain in the direction of Buttons. It was dark. The rain was steady, but the air was not rough. The windshield leaked, so our pant legs got wet, but that didn't bother us at all. That searchlight was a real worry, though. We had no idea whether we were being blown to the left or to the right; thus when we were about one hour out, we decided to go down low over the water in hope of seeing waves or land. Occasional breaks in the clouds gave us an occasional peek at the water, but we couldn't see it plain enough through our drift meter to determine any amount of wind effect. As we continued to use up our estimated time to the island, I kept feeding in just a little bit of right correction. There was a small mountain, about 3,000 feet high, on the north end of the island and that was on the left. As we were about 400 to 500 feet above sea level, the danger of getting close to that mountain became more and more apparent. No panic, yet, but plenty uncomfortable.

The rain became less severe, but we were still over water and we estimated our time was running out. It ran out. Still over water. Still no searchlight. I decided to overrun the same heading before admitting we were lost. As we edged close to the twenty minutes remaining, allocated by guess, we were all four with our noses forward and eyeballs looking harder than we had ever looked before. We had about two hours of fuel left and no place to go except to that searchlight. At ETA, plus twenty minutes, we started our search pattern of circling left with gradually increasing circles. We were hoping to see any shoreline for a more favorable place to ditch if necessary or the light beam or anything except the 3,000 foot high mountain. Before we completed the first circle at about 500 feet altitude, there, just outside the window by my left elbow, was that beautiful searchlight. It could hardly be seen in the rain and I bet only shone through about 1,000 feet of clouds instead of 20,000, as the guy had told me. But the field was also about twenty minutes or about fifty miles farther than planned and definitely off to the left some distance. It was a pretty sight at just about midnight. Chalk up another for Saint Christopher.

Other members of our squadron in New Guinea weren't so lucky. On November 10, 1942, my good friend George Vandevort was taking a load of infantry from Port Moresby to Wanogela Mission across the Owen Stanley Range near Buna on the north side of New Guinea. He was in a mountain pass partially obscured by clouds when he ran into a mountain. Only the radio operator, Sergeant Kirschner, miraculously survived after spending thirty-eight days in the jungle. That made three planes and six men lost only twenty days after leaving the United States.

On another trip into Henderson Field during this very critical time for both the navy in the waters off the Solomons and the marines on land on Guadalcanal, a new service was inaugurated by the Thirty-third gooney birds. Apparently, on the twelfth and thirteenth of November (from my Form 5 again) a single trip from Tontouta, to Buttons, to Cactus, to Roses (Efate), to Tontouta was required. Seventeen hours of flying time was too, too much. It's hard to recall just how tired, how weary, how beat a person could get under these circumstances, but the mission was very important and ended okay. We must have lived through it, because the Form 5 said we went back to Buttons on the fourteenth.

On that trip into Guadalcanal, we again arrived shortly before dark. My preference would have scheduled arrival time earlier in daylight, but the pace of battle in that area was still at its height. Planes from floating bases would go there to crash-land (not to fuel, because there was no fuel there). Japanese fighters and bombers were irregularly able to do damage to the strip, and the continuing naval battles were sometimes close to Guadalcanal and sometimes some distance away. The Japanese were pouring a lot of power into this fracas from their major base at Rabaul. So many ships from both sides had been sunk or put out of commission that no one could tell who might be the ultimate victor. The Japanese navy was larger, but ours was better.

Anyway, when we arrived and were unloaded, the marines pointed out a sight I shall never forget. Just off the strip, barely protected under some trees, was a line of wounded marines futilely awaiting evacuation to ships offshore that had some medical facilities aboard. Those ships were so loaded with casualties they just couldn't receive any more wounded. Besides, vessels capable of moving them from shore to ships were unavailable. Someone knew of a new tent hospital that was up, or partially up, at Efate (code name: Roses). I had never been there but knew where it was, about an hour southwest of Buttons. Buttons had only a dispensary. Roses had a strip with lights, fuel, and a field hospital under construction. It didn't take long to decide we should load some of those wounded and head for Roses. Because we still had four 100-gallon fuel tanks in the cabin, it was plain we couldn't load very many stretcher cases. The marine corpsman in charge of those horribly wounded men supervised getting a few stretcher cases aboard and also some that were able to sit. I saw and heard one stretcher case say just before they were to put him aboard, "Hey, I'll sit. That'll make room for about six more." He had a shoulder, part of his neck, and part of his upper arm blown off and was bandaged only with stripped clothing. There were no bandages. I wonder if he even had painkillers. Almost all the medicines and hospital supplies en route to Guadalcanal had been lost on the *Coolidge*. The corpsmen finally boarded all they could pack in, I'd guess about twenty-eight or thirty people. Probably eight were on stretchers. Not a moan or a groan was heard during loading. There were likely many sounds before the six-hour flight to Roses was completed. Those guys were tough. And great. I love the marines. Even today, forty-eight years later, I weep when I think of those helpless wounded, so many of them.

It was four days before we got back to Guadalcanal. That was because we were not permitted to use the airstrip. If conditions were any tighter than during those three days, it's hard to imagine how they could have been. How could there be any more crucial events than during the past two weeks? Historians agree that the month of November 1942 was the period when our navy in the Solomons began to get the upper hand. There was more Japanese tonnage on the bottom at Iron Bottom Bay than there was American.

I was back into Guadalcanal on November 18. This was probably the time Gen. Alexander Vandegrift, commanding officer of the marines, hitched a ride in. They, the marines, didn't yet have their air transport in the area, if they had it at all. Later, they had the Marine Air Transport Command. Since they widely used C-47s, one would have to presume the general liked what he saw in our small effort. But he never did write any letter about it.

I'd prefer to recall that the general told me that things were beginning to look a little brighter and that our side would soon begin to push back the Japanese area and line of control, but I can't stretch the truth quite that far. However, in the following week or so we seemed to pick up more rumors that the battle for the Solomons was about over. We also heard rumors, or started some, that significant reinforcements would be coming into Tontouta and that this might be an auspicious time for our five crews to head out for Australia and on to New Guinea to join the rest of our squadron.

Because we had no written orders keeping us in the Solomon area, we surely didn't need any definite orders, verbal or written, in order to sneak off to Brisbane. That's what we decided we would do just as soon as we were sure that several contingents of reinforcements had arrived at Tontouta.

We could truly say we had worked alongside such heroes as Halsey, Vandegrift, General Holcomb, and pilots such as Pappy Boyington, Joe Foss, and Indian Joe Bauer (who was shot down and killed in aerial combat over Henderson Field on November 14, 1942).

Several years later the world learned that part of the success of our outnumbered and outgunned navy over the Japanese navy in the Solomon area was again due to the ingenuity and expertise of the U.S. troops fighting vigorously in defense of our country. Some intelligence people in a radio facility somewhere had, for the first time, broken a major Japanese secret code and were intercepting the operational orders regarding the deployment of their vessels and ground forces. Our commanders were then able to meet most of their new landing forces with well-placed and organized troops of our own. The Japanese would try a new location, and by golly, the marines would be there waiting for them. The same things were happening to their naval forces. The Japanese interpreted this strong defense to mean that the marine forces were much larger and better equipped than they really were. Thanks to the guys who came up with ULTRA, the code breaker.

Just before the end of November a sizable contingent of reinforcements began arriving at Tontouta. That was our agreed upon sign to get out of this hellhole. We fueled up and refused to let anyone put supplies aboard. We came from wherever we were to PDG. The next morning, November 28, bright and early, we took off singly and headed for Brisbane.

The contingent that arrived at Tontouta brought a big bunch of new people. New faces were everywhere in that limited space. There is a saying, "imagine my surprise." Imagine mine when I heard one of them holler out, "Hey, George, is that you?" It came from Alan Fryberger, the piano-playing genius of Charlo, Montana. He claimed he was a propeller specialist. Baloney. Those ground grippers just needed music for fun and formality, so within the membership of the authorized Tables of Organization they inserted enough qualified musicians whose secondary duty was "Band." A year or two later, I saw Alan again, performing in his secondary duty in a fine, large military jazz band. Several of his mates were, or had been before the war, professional musicians with name bands. They made up a fine military band and gave much pleasure to those who heard them.

We presumed the actual line of demarcation between the South Pacific Command under Admiral Halsey and Southwest Pacific Command under General MacArthur would be the halfway line between New Caledonia and Australia. Since we estimated a six-and-a-half-hour flight to Brisbane, that line should be three and a quarter hours out of PDG. When we reached the halfway point and had not been shot down for being AWOL or some other criminal act, we set up a joint holler: "So long, Solomons; hello, Brisbane!" We presumed we'd get billeted in a nice metropolitan hotel, with baths and food from a menu and handshakes of congratulation from dignitaries for a piece of a job well one. Nope. We landed at Amberly Field and were told to go right on to Archer Field and then on to Port Moresby tomorrow morning, November 25, 1942. So much for the bright lights of a big city outside the combat zone.

Chapter 8
New Guinea

Phase I

Go to Port Moresby! Right now! That seemed to be the duty at hand, but again it was hard to figure out who was supposed to be giving orders, verbal or written. Somehow the CO (Commanding Officer) of the Thirty-third was billeted in Townsville, Australia, which was like a suboffice of MacArthur's Brisbane headquarters. The aircrews who were up in Port Moresby (Papua New Guinea) were doing the best they could to establish a campsite at Ward's Airdrome without any legitimate source of supplies or any ground echelon to organize the effort. Their job was to fly every day.

During our overnight stay in Townsville, we were briefed about the overall situation and the general plan of action that was then current. It was very informative, because we knew nothing of the action taking place in Australia or New Guinea.

The military situation wasn't exactly rosy anywhere in the Pacific. MacArthur had personally evacuated his headquarters from the Philippines in a PT boat successfully. This in itself is a story of luck, grit, and talent. Some U.S. aircraft from the Philippines, but not many, had flown to Australia via Java. They had gathered together enough fighter aircraft with pilots and stationed them at Darwin, where the Japanese ultimate plan of attack on the Aussie mainland would most likely take place. A few bombers were scrounged from friends in that part of the world, but again, not in numbers enough to really organize. The U.S. air combat pilots and planes in the Philippines had fought on as great heroes but were almost totally eliminated. Several transport-type planes that had been used in MacArthur's retreat were in Australia and had been put to good use within a new organization under General Kenney.

By this time two squadrons, or portions thereof, had been formed from those available aircraft into the Twenty-first and Twenty-second transport squadrons. Talk about a hodgepodge! They had about one each of the following type aircraft: L-4, C-56, DC-5, DC-2, B-17, and one DC-3. When we arrived as a bona fide troop carrier squadron they threw us all together, from an administration standpoint, as the 374th Troop Carrier Group. We were then under the command of Gen. George Kenney, who was MacArthur's chief of air. Those makeshift units, the Twenty-first and Twenty-second, had already flown a bunch of the U.S. Thirty-second Infantry Division from Australia to Port Moresby. The first half of our Thirty-third Squadron had been at Port Moresby for the better part of the month of November 1942. During that time, our half was detained for the Guadalcanal affair. We spent the one night, November 30, 1942, in Townsville and then joined the rest of the Thirty-third at Port Moresby.

The Thirty-third Ground Echelon was on the high seas with our supplies and equipment. Again we were to be orphans, without the necessary people and material to keep our planes in the air and the crew members in adequate health. It was a joyous reunion that afternoon with the other part of our air echelon, because they had acquired several tents, staked out a place in the brush to call our bivouac area, and found some other U.S. units that had field kitchens with cooks. That meant we got to fill our mess kits with whatever delicacy they would be serving that night. Even the two fresh-air latrines that had been established looked pretty good.

By the time we had exchanged greetings and unloaded our gear, the Aussies came along with trucks of supplies and piled them into any plane with an open cargo door, saying they were urgently needed "over the hump," where the Yanks and the Aussie ground forces were locked in very critical jungle combat with the Japanese. So I made my first trip to New Guinea on my first afternoon in the theater. Then we also got more bad news. The Thirty-third had lost two more planes. As previously mentioned, one plane was piloted by my good friend George Vandevort and carried a crew of two and about twenty-five fully equipped infantry soldiers. The other plane was piloted by S. Sgt. Marvin Brandt, with a crew of three and unknown cargo aboard.

Five weeks out of the United States, and we had lost four of our thirteen aircraft and eleven crew members. Not good.

Overall, the situation was that the Japanese had been able to move forward in the entire theater because of having a vastly superior navy (in numbers). This was because they had been preparing for an aggressive war for several years. They had a large ground force, well equipped, and their strategy was well conceived and at first well executed toward their goal of controlling the entire Pacific, including Indonesia, China, and Australia. They had had easy going, so far, on their thrust southward, but they failed to consider the abilities and dedication of the entire U.S. population. Especially the military. We didn't take kindly to being hit mercilessly by purportedly friendly nations while their official ambassadorial representatives stood in their silk trousers and long-tailed jackets before their counterparts in our nation's capitol and declared that Japan had no intention of initiating any aggressive action against the United States. Remember that. And remember Pearl Harbor. And don't feel the least bit guilty about Hiroshima.

The Japanese had advanced rapidly through the Philippines, Indonesia, the Solomon Islands, and New Guinea. At the South Pacific Command in Nouméa, Halsey said, "No more." In Australia, MacArthur was willing to concede the top (north) one-third of the country, but no more. That was known as "the Mac-Arthur line." But he really didn't want to give it away. So he didn't. Since he now had the U.S. Thirty-second Infantry Division on hand

and the Forty-first Division on the way, he conceived and implemented a new military concept. First, stop the enemy from advancing farther. Second, counterpunch by interrupting their resupply lines. Third, control a limited number of key strategic staging areas. Fourth, don't waste too much time and don't commit all of our resources to each enemy stronghold. Fifth, move around or over to the next place we want to develop as a strong base of operation. In other words, don't fight for every foot of sea and jungle—play leapfrog. Hold the line.

We moved forward and toward our objective—the Philippines. We cut off the Japanese supply lines and starved them out. We didn't care how long that would take. Because of brilliant execution of that plan and the arrival of adequate troops and equipment from the rapidly expanding industrial output of the U.S.A., the leapfrog plan worked real well.

Port Moresby in 1942 was not the average key logistical city as we knew such cities back on the mainland. There was a main road from the port to the airport, used mainly by military trucks that hauled equipment and supplies, which arrived by boat, out to the airplanes. From this point the supplies could go on to those places most in need. Actually, a limited number of cargo vessels arrived at the port at this stage, probably because the Japanese had gotten to within thirty miles of the town. I think the few defending Aussies, as well as the advancing enemy infantry, presumed that Moresby would fall. It didn't. The Aussie infantry held them back around Kokoda, which was near the top of the Owen Stanley Mountains, which divided the sea to the north from the sea to the south. Our troop carrier planes carried the U.S. Thirty-second and Forty-first divisions over the heads of the advancing Japanese foot soldiers to port villages along the northern coast of Papua.

This was the beginning of the leapfrog experiment. We landed engineers and troops at such places as Wanigela Mission, Buna, Pongani, and some open spaces that a load of engineers would pick from the window. The *kunai* grass would be as much as five feet tall, but it wasn't thick, so we could tell from the air that the ground was not rocky, sorta level, no gully crossing through it, and long enough to be able to stop. The dust would fly, we would stop, and the cargo door would open. Then the engineers would manhandle their jeep down the ramp. They'd grab their rifles and radio gear and head for the jungle. Some of those clearings actually became usable strips for follow-up delivery of men and equipment. One area was a nice long valley about half way between Kokoda and Buna that became a major staging area even while the battles for Buna and Kokoda were still going on. Ultimately two long strips were built there and remain until this day. They were named Dobodura and Popondetta.

The Aussies had been administrators of Papua for quite some time, and because there were no roads they had developed a number of small landing strips throughout the country. Those landing strips became very important to us and to the infantry forces, because our good old C-47s could land and take off from a number of those small strips. However, our engineering battalions could not get any dirt-moving equipment in, so they had to hire native "Fuzzy-Wuzzies," who somehow got those strips lengthened and broadened. We hauled in a lot of steel runway, interlocking matting, that had come to Port Moresby by ship. That is how landing strips were built and how the infantry was delivered to the front lines. Likewise, that's how food and equipment were made available and how wounded (and worse) were taken back to civilization.

When our half of the squadron arrived at Ward's Airdrome, Port Moresby, the entire north shoreline of Papua New Guinea was under entrenched Japanese control. This territory included all the area betwixt Milne Bay on the extreme east end of New Guinea, along the hogback line of the Owen Stanley Mountains to Dutch New Guinea, and then all of that country.

Actually, Port Moresby was not too secure. We all had dug slit trenches near our tents and along the revetment areas where the planes were parked or worked on when not in the sky. At this time the enemy air attacks on our base were infrequent. But anything of ours on the other side of the Owen Stanleys was regularly subject to both air and ground attack. Although Port Moresby was classified a combat area, we had to fly into the area across the mountains controlled by the enemy in order for it to be classified a combat mission. Since our planes were unarmed, our only defense in the air was to "go like hell" when Zeros were spotted nearby. We would get down low—I mean like in the trees—and head for home. The Zeros didn't like to dive down low. It put them in jeopardy in case some U.S. P-39s or P-40s were in the area. Our fighter pilots were so much superior to the Japanese, we troop carrier guys felt quite secure when the fighters were covering for us. We did still have one Thompson submachine gun aboard, and I always carried my .45 pistol.

Our living conditions were quite a bit below minimum low standards. It was hot, humid, sweaty, dusty, muddy, lonesome, busy, uncertain, and sometimes downright discouraging. Offsetting our own discomfort was the appreciation and thanks of the infantry troops, who really had it rotten. They sometimes lived for days in swamps, in thick jungle, or on barren hillsides, with very little food and nearly always the sound of enemy fire not too far away. Their casualty rate was quite high, killed, wounded, or psycho. But somehow their overall morale seemed high. They seemed to know they had a job to do. They were doing theirs better than the enemy was doing his, and besides, they had a score to settle: "Remember Pearl Harbor? They can't get away with that." As more supplies and personnel came along, everyone felt stronger and just a little more certain we were ultimately going to win.

Stress and strain were everywhere. On the ground, in the air, both night and day. I recall feeling tired and weary at the end of one flying day and sharing some concerns with George Schnieders. As we didn't yet have our own mess hall, we just nibbled at C rations and had a visit. A mess hall wouldn't have been much better than the C rations we carried anyway. I mentioned that I didn't feel too sharp. I was getting careless with my pilot duties. For example, sometimes I would have the plane ready to land while still six or eight feet in the air; other times the ground would hit me before I was ready. George said, "I'm sure as hell glad to hear you say that. I'm having the same troubles." We talked about it and actually decided that we had to improve our mental attitude (keep our chins up, you know). To bootstrap our disposition upward, we did some physical exercise regularly. Also, we showered every day. We would build a shower by hanging a couple of fighter plane belly tanks in a tree and get a water trailer to fill them. We even quit taking Atabrine because it affected our equilibrium and that's why those planes wouldn't land properly. We actually got quite enthused about our plan. A pair of good Catholic boys could keep the faith. We would throw in a little Christian Science for health reasons, and by bathing more, we'd smell better and laugh more. By not taking Atabrine we wouldn't turn yellow, and in spite of that we never, ever caught malaria. The planes behaved properly, and we both became great pilots (in our opinion). I can almost say, speaking for myself, that I didn't have another uneasy moment, except in an emergency or a crisis, thereafter. But perhaps that is stretching it some.

The arrival of the ground echelon of the Thirty-third in late December 1942 was a most welcome occasion. They had been on the high seas for a lot of days, so the fact of having a "home" was exciting to them. They didn't even care very much about the real discomforts caused by bivouac living. They had a medical doctor, field kitchens, jeeps, airplane parts, a mechanical cadre, a radio department, engineering, pencil and paper pushers, extra pilots, extra flying personnel, and a gung-ho attitude of wanting to get to work. They also had a CO; thus a power fight began between the two COs. Both were captains, neither had much command experience (but more than the rest of us), and both had clean uniforms. Finally the original CO, Jackson, sent word up to New Guinea that he was the officer in charge and Ward went back to the States. I never did see Ward.

One of the many good things about the people in the newly arrived ground echelon was the new bunch of staff sergeant pilots. Fully qualified and a credit to the Air Corps. I'll never know why they were made staff sergeant pilots instead of officers. The rank didn't make diddly difference in New Guinea except on occasions when a traveling visitor from the mainland would come by and slight our noncommissioned flying pilots. We seldom wore rank insignia anyway. In fact, we didn't have time to realize rank was a part of military discipline until much later. Maybe we were so dirty we all looked the same. I especially recall Wylie, Bruce, Patterson, and Nabors. As pilots there were none better. As good guys they were exceptional. Any time there was one more flight to be made, marginal weather, or an unusually dangerous trip, they would be among the first to volunteer.

Then there was Pappy Sexton, line chief. He was overseer of the crew chiefs. Pappy was exceptionally innovative in many of the gray areas of getting the job done, which weren't provided for in the normal course of fighting a war. For example, as a squadron, we were always short of transport. Not so for Pappy. It wasn't long before he was driving around in an unmarked jeep that he kept parked by his tent with a full tank of gas. This jeep even had a top on it to keep out the sun and rain and had a switch that only Pappy could turn on. A couple of us looked at it closely one day and swore we could see under the paint job just a faint indication of the word NAVY. I wouldn't be surprised if Pappy took that jeep home with him.

Once when one of our planes took a few marine fighter pilots to New Zealand for a couple of days of R & R, Pappy went along as crew chief. When these mini vacations ended, the crew and passengers would often be in various stages of poor health—perhaps from bad water, but definitely hungover. When it was time for Pappy's group to return, the crew and passengers were somehow

General Kenney pinning the first of five Distinguished Flying Cross awards on Lieutenant Wamsley

rounded up and the pilot lucked out and got the plane off the ground, headed toward Australia. He asked Pappy to come and sit in his seat while he went back to sleep. Not long after that, the copilot fell asleep, so Pappy woke him and told him to go back and take a nap. Pappy was alone up front. One of the marine fighter pilots who was mobile came on up and sat in the copilot's seat. They visited some about the plane, the instruments, and the good time in New Zealand and then got around to where each of them was from. The marine told of his combat flying experiences in Guadalcanal and how he learned to fly. Then he asked Pappy, "Where'd you go to flying school?"

Pappy said, "I didn't."

"Oh. Where'd you learn to fly?"

"I don't know how," said Pappy.

Sgt. "Pappy" Sexton and Lieutenant Wamsley christening the first washbasins and garbage can at Ward's Airdrome, Port Moresby

"Well, are you a pilot?"

"No, I'm not."

"Can you land this airplane?"

"I doubt it; I've never tried. Doesn't make much difference anyway. I don't know where we're going or how to get there. I'm just a mechanic."

"Holy Christ!" said the marine. "I'm going back and have a few more drinks."

Blessed be the blind, for they shall sometimes be led. They got back.

Over the next few months, things more or less settled into a daily routine around our camp area and our work from Five Mile Strip became less hectic. At least that's where I think we were. Having almost the full complement of personnel called for in the Table of Organization made some order out of the chaos experienced earlier in the war zone. We had more flying people on call, and because of the combat situation, pilots were required to be always available to haul the merchandise and the troops to their next destination. The Australians provided most of the equipment and supplies while the Yanks furnished the combat troops. The aborigines worked for the Aussies loading trucks from the docks and then moving the supplies into the airplanes. The natives were very loyal and dependable, but they didn't speak or understand much plain English. They used a pidgin English that would make a few words understandable. They smelled pretty bad, but they always seemed happy—probably because they were high from the betel nuts they constantly chewed.

We would have an occasional daytime air raid and afterward have a single plane spend some time overhead at night just to aggravate us. It was Washing-Machine Charlie all over again. We had no antiaircraft guns. Three pistol or rifle shots in the middle of the night signaled the approach of enemy aircraft overhead and served as our notice to hit the slit trench. We became pretty casual about the need to take cover, especially if we thought it was a single plane that rarely even dropped one bomb.

During December of 1942, I flew forty-three combat missions; in January of 1943, twenty-one; and February of 1943, thirty-six. We all had a steady job. The clouds would start building over the Owen Stanleys about 11:00 A.M. and be too rough to fly through by about 2:00 P.M. and too high to fly over. Sometimes coming back from the other side we'd go as high as 18,000 or 20,000 feet without oxygen, but only for a short while. If the copilot started acting funny it was time to get low and get him some thicker air to breathe right away. The pilots didn't act funny.

This period was a bad time for the infantry. They were sloshing onward through jungle and swamp, but at least reinforcements came in regularly. Our ground troops didn't take many prisoners, even though the intelligence people in Brisbane were constantly sending messages asking that a few be sent there for interrogation. We occasionally hauled some back but didn't like the idea of having them aboard any more than the troops liked shepherding them to a pickup point. Those Japanese were suicidal. We heard stories of them hiding a grenade in their crotch or armpit with the idea of taking some Yanks along with them to their ancestors. Our boys always gave them a strip search before tying them up.

At about this time, there were some spectacular dogfights within our general area of operations. New units of heavy bombers indicated someone back in the States had decided our theater of activity had better have some help or the western Pacific area would be handed over to the enemy. Three additional runway strips had been built in the Port Moresby area, and two more were planned. We Thirty-third pilots and crews were glad to see additional P-39 and P-40 fighters arrive, because they were flying cover for us regularly. Fighter escort planes were available to the bombers and to us at some locations we flew into. These fighter escorts knocked down a lot of enemy planes, but more seemed to come to take their place.

These loyal natives could carry heavy loads.

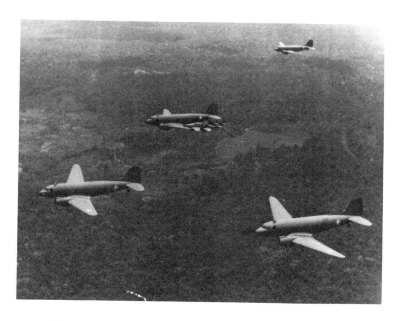

On the way to deliver troops and supplies, New Guinea

One of the wildest dogfights I ever witnessed was over Milne Bay, at the extreme east end of New Guinea. There must have been sixty or eighty Japanese bombers being escorted by seventy-five to one hundred Zeros. I don't know the exact numbers, but it was a bunch. I also don't know how our side got so many fighters in the air either. I'd guess there were at least forty or fifty. Our planes and pilots were again superior. They picked up the large enemy formation only a few miles from Milne Bay harbor, and the fight was on. Planes began to fall out of the sky in every direction. They were nearly all enemy that day. So many of their bombers were knocked down at the very first part of the attack that the remaining bombers didn't complete their bomb run. They turned and headed back for Rabaul. Sitting on the ground, I saw with my own eyes at least thirty planes go down. I think we lost only four fighters. Can you imagine that? Score: thirty to four. I remember thinking I'd bet the folks back home would not believe the figures if they made the papers. That was not an uncommon ratio. Our guys were good. And the Japanese were beginning to realize it. But they were pushing hard on many fronts. They wanted Port Moresby.

Milne Bay was one prong in their thrust. Another was the Wau/Bulolo area just a few miles inland from Lae. Wau seemed an unlikely spot to fight for. The town had fewer than 100 natives. There was no road to anywhere except a dirt trail back toward Lae. It was on the Japanese side of the mountains, and there was no way to punch a road over to our side. The airstrip was good for only the lightest of planes and of course the C-47s.

Wau Strip has been described as one of the world's oddest. It had mountains on three sides, so once you decided to land, you landed. There was no going around for another look. The strip was about 3,000 feet long, and the front end was 300 feet lower in elevation than the back end. So it was easy to land after the first time: Just cross the stream and drive the gear into the ground. When the plane slows down, which it will real fast, gun it so you can taxi to the upper end. Turn sideways, put the brakes on, and let the guys

George Wamsley beside trusty C-47 in New Guinea, 1942

(mostly Aussies) open the door and jump to the ground ready to fight.

Lots of times we didn't even stop the engines. When the crew chief closed the door, we goosed the engines, turned downhill, and headed for home. Regular pilots don't believe it, but I have pictures.

The Schwensen Incident

In January of 1943, the Japanese were reinforcing their ground troops approaching Wau by bringing in supplies and personnel over a mountain trail on foot. We had been bringing in additional Aussie troops regularly during the month, because the Japanese were getting close to the Wau airstrip and our side was not about to give them any more ground. On February 6, the Japanese were in control of one side of the creek at the foot of the airstrip and the Aussies had control of the other side and the 500 or 600 yards up to and including the airstrip.

I left Port Moresby at about 10:00 A.M. with a load of ammunition and hand grenades and a one-star Australian brigadier. I was leading a three-plane flight with Schwensen on my left wing. The general had asked if he could hop a ride to run up and see how his boys were doing. I agreed and he stood between me and the copilot for quite awhile and then went back to look out the side windows. The only place he had to sit was on the wooden boxes containing the ammo and the grenades. Those boxes had no covers— they were just open boxes.

It was much smarter to go toward Wau at a rather low altitude, staying out of the high mountains on our side until we came to a pass that we could take and still remain at a level below the mountaintops. If you didn't know the right pass to enter by sight, you'd get partway into a wrong pass and then run out of space, requiring a quick turnaround. That turnaround was easy enough for a single plane if you saw the end of the pass coming toward you, but there wasn't really enough room to turn around a formation.

Japanese fighter and bomber planes had been making sporadic small-volume attacks on Wau and Bulolo for some time, but not every day. Those distractions were frequent enough that we had learned to approach Wau as low as possible in order to not give enemy fighters an easy shot at us. A three-plane formation could slip out the end of the pass, lower gear, spread out, and hit the end of the runway with as little exposure as possible. Three planes were about all the strip could handle at one time anyway. It was our planes the Japanese were after, because we were carrying either more troops or supplies.

Just before we reached the opening into the small Wau valley, two Japanese Zeros came out of the clouds directly in front of me. Our fighter cover was four P-40s low and four high. They would sweep back and forth with the lead pair moving off to the side while the trailing pair was directly overhead and slightly behind. Our four low-cover group was just making a pass overhead when I saw the two Zeros directly in front and pointed straight at us and not very far away. They were firing. We could see the tracers going by. I didn't have much leeway to go down any lower but took every inch available—right then. The nose went down and the tail went up until we were practically in the creek. The creek was narrow, but we were not a very good target. I looked over to see Schwensen, who had been six or ten feet off my left wing when the Zeros showed up, but he wasn't in sight. The other C-47 who was on my right was turning off to the right, and he appeared to be about ten feet above tree level also.

The lead P-40 plane passing overhead was past the line of the Zeros and didn't get a shot off on this pass. His wingman, Danacher, I think, was trailing just enough that with instant reaction he was able to get off a short burst of about forty rounds. He knocked down one Zero. I stayed creek-high, passed the end of the airstrip, and went on toward Bulolo. Must have stayed quite low, because I recall on some sharp turns I'd watch the wing tip to make sure it didn't touch water. My copilot, Sergeant Johnson, was looking out the windows the best he could and hollering an excited blow-by-blow report on the dogfight going on.

About that time, the brigadier nudged between the crew chief and radio operator, who were leaning over the pilot seats trying to see whatever they could, and asked, "Will we be landing pretty soon? It's awfully rough in the back end, and those crates are flying all over the cabin." He didn't feel too well. I had forgotten about him being aboard. When I finally saw those cases scattered all over the cabin I realized he must have had a pretty rough ride back there. We got downstream, probably five miles, got behind a ridge and over the mountains, and headed home without delivering our load.

I think six Japanese planes were shot down and we lost one P-40 and one C-47. We assumed that the second Zero got Schwensen.

On October 8, 1988, forty-six years later, an Associated Press dispatch from Port Moresby told of the finding of the wreckage of Schwensen's plane buried in a hillside about two miles from Wau. In the dispatch the plane was properly identified, the crew was properly named, and the circumstances of the finding were explained. A team of specialists in recovery and identification procedures was immediately sent from Hawaii to map the crash site and determine the feasibility of recovery. They traveled from Lae to Wau by jeep and then to the crash area by helicopter. They spent four miserable days during heavy rain on a steep mountainside using shovels, brooms, and hand brushes, locating, recovering, and mapping each fragment found.

The remains of the five crew members were returned to the U.S. Army Central Identification Laboratory in Hawaii for identification. That lab does extensive analysis and reporting on such casualties. These men perform a very unpleasant task in a very conscientious manner. The final report on each individual was sixty to eighty pages on the various stages of the process. Data was recorded, signed over, forwarded on, followed up, analyzed, summarized, and closed out by the proper authorities. Many signatures by high-ranking people and several committees' reports resulted in positive identification of each individual. Seems like a lot of effort, but any surviving kin must be completely satisfied that those remains of so long ago are really those of the lost family member.

The locating of next of kin or other surviving family members was not easy. I felt our Thirty-third Squadron people would be a good source of that information, so I got in touch with Arizona's fine congressman, John McCain, and he immediately gave me the number of the man in charge in Washington who handled that problem. That person, a Mr. Manning, wanted all the help he could get but hesitated about giving us a free hand to handle the situation. After all, it was his job and sometimes the next of kin have other axes to grind with the government or the military and need special treatment.

Within two weeks of the news item, I had received eight or ten phone calls from our squadron people from all parts of the United States. (We don't have very many members left.) So we set about finding remaining family members. I acted as the clearinghouse. Between us and Manning, we located one 94-year-old mother and at least one family member for each of the casualties.

These were the crewmen:

Schwensen: Lieutenant pilot, Kansas. His wife had remarried (and has grandkids). One brother lives in California, and another lives in Texas. Two other brothers were killed in WW II in the European theater.

Sherman: Lieutenant copilot, New York City. One brother lives in Pennsylvania.

Erickson: Corporal radio operator, Minnesota. One brother lives in Minnesota.

Fawn: Private crew chief, Ohio. His mother was still alive in Ohio at the time of the burial ceremonies; she died a short time after the funeral. Six brothers and sisters living. Four brothers and sisters deceased.

Piekutowski: Private, first class, assistant crew chief, Michigan. One brother lives in South Dakota. One sister lives in Wisconsin.

The positive identification took almost a full year to accomplish, and by then all relatives were located and notified.

Newspaper stories and TV interviews in the home states of the victims gave the incident wide coverage. After all, it was a long time between the deaths and the burials. Lieutenant Sherman was buried in Arlington with full military honors. The three enlisted men were also buried in Arlington, but in a single casket. Their remains were so intermingled in the rear of the airplane that individual caskets didn't seem proper. Lieutenant Schwensen was buried beside his brothers at the Fort Leavenworth, Kansas, military cemetery in an elaborate ceremony. The funeral included an old C-47 flying over the parade route and a missing man flyby with some modern jet aircraft.

I made quite a few new friends among those families. Two different ones wanted nothing to do except close the book on their "presumed dead" family member. I was trying to make up an album about each individual and needed old pictures and news reports. After letters and phone calls and boxes of See's chocolates, everyone responded as best they could. I took the album to our latest squadron reunion, in Wichita, Kansas, and it was well received. I recently talked to an officer from the U.S. air base in Frankfurt, Germany, who had seen the coverage of the events in his base newspaper. He said, "You guys were great. You were pioneers and heroes, and you made some history. The air force is proud of you."

About this time, February 1943, we were sending twelve planes in a single formation with lots of fighter cover on every mission. The squadron CO occasionally wanted to lead the flight. Okay, rank has its privileges. On this particular flight, as we approached the area to go through the mountains, he turned into a dead-end canyon, which the rest of us knew about. There was strict radio silence, because we were close to the Japanese air base at Salamaua, thus we couldn't warn him. The rest of us knew that there would be no way to turn that formation around at the altitude we were entering. So we all moved up a little higher and higher, where there would be more room to maneuver when turning back. The CO found himself quite alone. There was no danger being low down in the canyon for a single plane, but when he saw his eleven other planes quite a bit higher and falling back, he asked over the radio, "What's going on here?" A voice came back that some of us recognized as Glotzbach; he was singing a hymn. "Where he leads me, I will follow—unless it's into a dead-end canyon." Our CO was mortified.

We had now lost, out of the original thirteen planes and fifty-two crewmen, five planes and sixteen crewmen. We had been out of the U.S.A. for only 109 days. The places we were hauling to principally at this time included: Wau, Bulolo, Pongani, Gona, Milne Bay, Kokoda, Dobodura, Popondetta, and Thirty Mile. I'm sure there were others.

Phase II

A little later on. Indefinite time frame, but generally after the first two months working out of Port Moresby, March 1943.

By now we started getting into longer trips. There was more fighter cover available to us, and because of that cover the enemy had fewer planes at their bases that were nearest Port Moresby. They had taken some losses from our heavy bombers at their bases a bit farther out. The U.S. Navy was beginning to score some victories by hit-and-run tactics. This meant that neither side had a well-defined forward line. This was more of Doug's leapfrog plan.

We would occasionally fly past an area that was really held by the Japanese, but frequently our Navy had landed troops on another island off the coast or even between two bases on the New Guinea coast, so the Japanese paid less attention to us. Oftentimes we could see just a few planes on their landing strips. But frequently, because of our fighter cover, they wouldn't come up after us. I imagine they were sometimes short of fuel, too.

General Kenney occasionally stopped by our operations office to "b.s." about what we had seen coming into those enemy airfields in the late afternoon, because our visual sightings were up-to-date and other communications were nonexistent. If a goodly number of enemy fighter planes were coming into a particular field, the general would see that his B-25s, medium bombers, would be in there the next morning at daybreak. From treetop height they would drop fragment bombs and incendiaries on the Zeros and Bettys lined up side by side. I guess the Japanese didn't want to go on a mission until their breakfast had settled. General Kenney's tactics were very effective. They'd wipe out many planes on the ground and rarely lost a B-25. The B-25s would even do a couple of repeat jobs on the same strip a few days later.

About this time, we got more into the drop business. Small isolated groups—usually Australians—who would be working their way through the jungle on foot would somehow get a message out that they were hungry and thirsty. They would identify a small opening with a white "X," which meant they were nearby and wanted (read that: *needed*) supplies dropped there ASAP. Usually we would go in with one plane, find the "X," sneak through the gullies, and have the guys in the back push out bags and boxes of supplies. When those groceries hit the ground at 125 miles per hour, the bags and boxes would break, spreading the provisions over a wide area. That wasn't too good for the guys on the ground, because they would be exposed while picking up the groceries, in case any were in pieces big enough to pick up.

Later on, small parachutes were attached to the packages; this method delivered the goods in much better shape than previously. That is, if the pilot rang the bell signaling "push" at the proper time. I've seen some of those ground people run out into the open before we dropped, waving their mess kits wildly about, signaling that they were really hungry. Even if they knew the Japanese were close by, they would stay in the clearing while we made our passes over and shoved out the packages. Some of them had to have been hurt by the flying bully beef and jelly.

Drop Mission near Salamaua Strip

A good-looking white-haired bird colonel had brought a replacement squadron of troop carriers to Townsville. They would be coming to Moresby in a few days, and he wanted to find out what we were doing and how we did it. He didn't really know what our mission was at this time. He asked to fly copilot with me for a day to see something of how we worked. We were going to drop a load at a site that I had found and dropped at a few days earlier. We would drop, if the white cloth was visible, on a very small clearing in a rather deep gully about 1,000 feet lower than the nearby surrounding mountains. This was about two miles from the Salamaua strip. Salamaua was an operating Japanese fighter-plane base, and the Aussie patrol we were dropping to was in a position to see everything the enemy was doing there. The jungle was too thick and rugged for Japanese forces to make much of an effort to dislodge them.

The colonel climbed aboard as copilot. We did our usual two or three climbing circles to get altitude enough to get through to the other side through the Kokoda pass. We bore left down the mountains at treetop height and in and out of valleys and over ridges. As we approached Salamaua, where the mountains came quite close to the seashore, we hugged the hills real tight. We flew over the drop site and saw the white cloth. We had to go across ridge to ridge and crossed the drop site at almost 1,000 feet, which was much too high to drop. We tried to always drop at 100 feet or less.

At this site, we would have to drop going down the canyon, since there was no room to turn around going up the canyon. So we took a sharp left and climbed up through a saddle, which put us even higher than before. As we cleared the saddle, we had slowed down significantly but were headed downhill at about 1,500 feet above the drop site. We lowered the landing gear, let down some flaps, and throttled back to idle. A hard left turn put us at the head of the canyon and slowing down nicely. Another hard left and down the canyon we went, downhill, but not gaining very much speed because of the drag. We had to lose about 1,500 feet altitude in probably one mile, going downhill, to have an effective drop at treetop height, at stall speed.

As we approached the drop site, I rang the bell and the guys in the back pushed out the goodies. Some of them hit the target. We were planning to make three passes to get our cargo out. The colonel was a little bug-eyed at seeing this nonconventional use of an aircraft, but it was part of his job as copilot to also keep a sharp eye for bogey planes (unidentified aircraft) in the sky or for any sign of fighters taking off from Salamaua Strip. The few Zeros on the strip (maybe not operational) were the first enemy planes he got to see.

We made the second pass. As we got to the drop, a couple of Aussies gave us the thumbs up, meaning they would get at least some of the supplies we dropped. As we started up to the saddle for the third pass I said, "Okay, Colonel [I can't remember his name but have it written down somewhere], you do this one, and I'll ring the bell." I thought he would hesitate. Instead, he grinned a huge grin, grabbed the wheel, and hollered, "You bet!" He had me lower the gear and drop some flaps. Then he went through the saddle real slow and slid into the drop run without a quiver. I rang the bell. After we felt the load leave the rear end, I told him to turn right and head for home. He hugged the hills, right on the trees, and moved into and out of canyons, gradually ascending the side of the Owen Stanleys toward home. He knew where it was. And he was real smooth. When I asked him what kind of time he had this trip, he said, "I've had a great experience this morning. After many years as a pilot with American Airlines—I have almost 12,000 hours—I've never seen an airplane used like this one. I didn't think it could be done. But it sure as hell was fun." He decided it would be a good plan to have his inexperienced pilots fly with us for a few days before turning them loose on their own. He was a fine officer, a gentleman. The colonel stayed on in troop carriers in the area for some time. I never saw him again, but I know he didn't forget his first drop mission in New Guinea.

By now we had added several new places to fly into. First time into each was an adventure, because we had no tower and no map showing the exact location. We had no idea of the way to approach, and sometimes there would be dust you couldn't see through. From memory, I have picked a few of the names of these strips, and it would be hard to tell where the names came from: Lae, Nadzab, Finschhafen, Salamaua, Goodenough, Wau, Bulolo, Tsili-Tsili, Marilians, Pulpit, Amobea, Kiawna, Nunn's Point, Mount Hagen, Bitoi, Rorana, Gudagasal, Bena Bena, Skidawai, Moreba, Saputa, and Karema. We got to see a lot of natives from these villages. Many of them didn't even know that all those other native villages existed. Between those who knew their neighbors there were often tribal wars.

On April 12, 1943, the Japanese mounted one of their bigger raids on Port Moresby. This was only two months after their push on Wau had been stopped. One formation of about fifty Betty bombers, covered by about seventy-five Zeros, came toward Moresby in broad daylight. Our fighters picked them up near Thirty Mile, which was thirty miles from our strip. By the time the Japanese planes reached overhead, their formation was scattered and heading for home. I've seen movies since that didn't have nearly the action we watched that day. Many planes were shot down, but very few were ours. I say again, our guys and equipment were so much superior it was hard to believe. We, the Thirty-third, didn't lose a single plane that day.

The fact that the Japanese could muster that many aircraft for another unsuccessful raid indicated that everything wasn't going our way. Maybe that was why we had to fly so much. My trip records show:

March 1943
    14 trips to Wau
    22 trips to Dobodura
     6 trips to Skidawai
     6 trips to others
    48 trips total

April 1943
     7 trips to Wau
    22 trips to Dobodura
    16 trips to Skidawai
     6 trips to others
    51 trips total

This did not include the two or three trips to the mainland to Cairns, Townsville, and Darwin.

I remember a lot of things going on during that time. Some of them are worth recalling here. For instance, one time, a messenger came saying that three trucks would soon be arriving in our area and he asked, "Where do you want the engines unloaded?" We didn't have any new engines on order, but when someone said they were R-1800s (the kind we used—and needed) it didn't take long for some mechanics to find a hiding place back in the bush. Suddenly we had six brand-new engines available. I smelled the alert hand and skill of Pappy Sexton in this affair, but no one in our outfit ever gave away our secret. The engines weren't stolen, just stored away.

On some occasions, we would carry very valuable cargo over the hump to those poor guys of the Thirty-second and Forty-first divisions. Mail was the most priceless. Unfortunately, quite a bit of it would have to be hauled back. Other items that seemed as though they should be divided up a little more equitably included sugar, ham, canned fruit, jelly, spices, and other products not regularly available to the Yank cooks from the Australian quartermaster. So it wasn't unheard of, when such items were included in our cargo, that a few cases might be displaced and not unloaded at the destination. We also needed soap. Usually no big fuss was made of this procedure, but one day orders came down from higher authorities. We were to post the following directive on our bulletin board:

Dated: Day/Mo./Year
Effective 0600 hours one week from today there will be no more stealing of food from the airplanes.

Signed: Big Shot
Somewhere

Perhaps you can imagine the bountiful harvest of the next seven days. I did not wreck my airplane when taking off with five 100-pound sacks of sugar crammed into the small sanitary facility in the rear of the plane, but the tail hung so low the nose tried to go up. With alacrity, the proper countermeasures were applied, and we made it safely home.

Some time later, after hauling a load of plywood over the hill so a lowly one-star general could have some flooring in his tent and office, one of our more delinquent types got the idea we should have an officers' club. He thought we could requisition or steal the next load of flooring destined for someone else. We would hire some natives to build a thatched roof, and with a wood floor we would have a fine club. It came about, in time, exactly that way. There was very little booze, but benches and tables and occasional refreshments made it a quality operation.

One time (this part you don't have to believe) a one-star infantry general was hitchhiking from across the hill down toward the mainland for some personal R & R. He had to RON with us while waiting for a ride on the next segment of his journey. Most of us had gathered in our fine clubhouse for cheese and crackers and cards and stories. Naturally we were "KA-ing" the general, listening to his stories of horror and hardship, but also telling a few of our own. He mentioned how hard it was to get supplies. As if we didn't know. And do you know, he had "ordered flooring for two tents and two offices and some dirty bastards stole a good portion of it!" Probably Australian, he surmised. Funny looks passed around, but no one blinked and he never tumbled. He didn't know it, but his boots were on his flooring.

Speaking of improvisations, some were more practical than others. An unfortunate pilot, while taxiing his plane, had hooked a wing tip into a solid structure and ruined a good portion of the wing, making the plane unflyable. This plane was on an airstrip across the mountains, not accessible by road, and there was no chance of getting a new wing in by barge. It looked as if the plane would become unusable. Someone managed to gather enough manpower to roll it into the brush and gave it a good camouflage job so it couldn't be seen by Japanese aircraft. It was just kinda stored away for a while. The mechanics in our squadron couldn't stand to see a nearly working airplane just rotting away in the jungle. They started talking about ways to get a new wing over the mountain. They figured out a way to fasten an entire wing under one of their C-47s, fairing up the leading (butt) end so it wouldn't have too much air resistance. Then a pilot could just fly that mother across. There was some question of whether or not the gear would work up and down properly, but maybe some hot-shot pilot would fly it over the mountain without ever drawing up the landing gear.

By the time they acquired a whole wing, got the fairing tightly fastened thereto, and securely hung the wing under the frame of the plane, they had plenty of volunteers to haul it across. This unusual job got done, and the damaged plane was put back in service without further incident. I don't recall who finally flew the plane or just which of the mechanics went along to unfasten the load or even if they ever did raise the gear. I do remember that the plane used was Jayhawk, the one Glotzbach and Schwensen flew across from the United States. The reason I know it was Jayhawk is because I saw a picture of the C-47 with the wing attached hanging on the wall of a flying service office at Oakland Municipal Airport in 1987.

During this time, there were some unusual stories about personal experiences in that region of the world: A pilot somehow happened to see the word HELP spelled out on a hogback high up toward the top of the Owen Stanleys. By using a very small observation plane (an L-4 Cub, I think), he got up close enough to a small native village to determine that two Dutch missionaries were ill and needed to be evacuated to a hospital. They were carried to the small plane and brought to Moresby and properly placed in a small field hospital. These missionaries could speak some English and rapidly became pets of the American personnel because of the interesting stories they would tell. They had been in the outback living amongst the natives for over twenty years. During this period, they apparently had been out to civilization only three or four times, but they were of good cheer and good humor.

My favorite story developed when one of the missionaries, a little eighty-five-pound man, had been quite far afield from his normal sphere of ministering and was meeting new tribes of natives. On one occasion, he told us, he was to go to an adjoining tribe from wherever he was. Word was passed ahead that he would arrive there midday on the next day. With his walking staff and a couple of carrier boys, he arrived at the village. A village usually consisted of four or five thatch huts on the extreme hogback ridge, with valleys sloping off both sides. A path would be between the huts. When the missionary arrived, he met the natives, some twenty or thirty, including children, who lived on each side of the path. They were really dressed up. Properly so. A royal welcome for a visiting

It takes ingenuity to haul a replacement wing on the outside of an airplane—under the plane's belly!

dignitary. Of course, the natives don't wear any "Sunday" clothes in this area, but they do wear a headband and a belt and loincloth. Each of the natives had beautiful flowers in the headband and in the front of the belt. At a hand clap from the chief of the village, as the missionary walked between the lines, each native bowed his head. This was not in reverence, but to show him the beautiful flowers. He slowly walked by each one and admired the flowers and each individual. When he got to the end of the line, the excitement was high. It was an important and happy day. But the welcome was not yet over. The chief clapped twice, hollered a brisk command, "Abba-dabba-dabba," and the natives all turned around in unison, with their backs to the pathway.

The missionary saw more flowers when he was invited by the chief to retrace his steps between the rows of natives. As the missionary walked by, each native would bend over so the missionary could admire the bright, beautiful flowers firmly fastened between the cheeks of their arses. In relaying the story the missionary said, "I didn't laugh, as I was bursting to do, but made it to the end of the line after complimenting each individual. They were beautiful, friendly people. I lived with them for several weeks." He never seemed to tire of telling this story over and over to each American that would come by to see him, and he would hold his visitor's hand and smile and laugh all the while.

Another guy I remember was big, tall James C. (for Cunyas) Watson. Jim was convinced that if he lived through this fracas he would become one of the finest lawyers in his home state of Texas. He also felt that becoming a successful lawyer might possibly be the first step toward ultimately becoming governor of Texas. He had many of the attributes to take him at least that far. Jim always wore his .45 in a shoulder holster. He would read anything that became available, was a good speaker, and looked like he should be a politician just as he planned. He always carried a briefcase along on every trip. No one else ever did this except the generals' aides. Jim would never say just what he had in that briefcase, but we all presumed it was law books. It was heavy enough.

One time one of our gang saw Jim putting something in the case and said, "Hey, what's that you got in there?"

" 'Tain't none of your damn business. But I'll tell you what it is. It's sealed packages of food rations. As many packages as I can get in it. If I ever get shot down or lost in the jungle I'm gonna have some food along to keep me alive. And I'm not sharing with anyone. If you lazy guys won't take the trouble to take care of yourselves, who cares? Gimme your home addresses and I'll notify your parents." That darn Watson wanted to live just a little more than the rest of us, I guess. He must have really wanted to become governor.

Jim survived the war, went to a Texas law school, and became a good and prominent attorney. Unfortunately, Jim was killed in a head-on collision with a drunken driver who crossed over the lane as Jim was returning home after making a speech in another town. He never did get to be governor. Jim was a good friend.

Life wasn't all that comfortable for us. Jungle rot began to show up on quite a few people. It's a bit like athlete's foot, but isn't. Rot could pop out on hands, neck, feet, or anywhere, but Doc couldn't provide any fast cure. Sometimes it would go away for months and then return on a new part of the body. I had some rot under two fingernails when I came back Stateside that just wouldn't go away. My dad finally told me to use "Mentholatham" (his name for it). I kept some Mentholatum on those two fingers for a coupla weeks and have never had any jungle rot since.

Some progress in the upgrading of living conditions had been made by this time, but I can tell you, it wasn't the Waldorf Astoria!

All of our cots were properly covered with mosquito netting, which made for an almost bite-free night of sleep. Occasionally someone would tell of having been attacked by large mosquitoes while asleep because his knee or an elbow or his forehead was up against the netting. Malaria was quite common, but the Atabrine did an effective job of controlling the disease. However, not everyone took Atabrine and some of those did not contract malaria. George S. and I still did not take Atabrine, and neither one of us contracted the disease during our entire tour. Maybe we were just lucky.

By now there was a mess hall at Moresby. However, even the mighty officers were still served meals in their own mess kits after standing in line with anyone else who was being paid by the Allies. To get to the margarine one had to take a swipe across the top in one direction to remove the flies, followed by a deftly gauged backswing to dig out the desired amount of grease. There must have been a bakery somewhere close by, because we occasionally saw a cook come by carrying a load of unwrapped bread piled up on his sweaty, hairy chest. At first we didn't eat the crust because of the way he carried around the loaves. Later on, this didn't seem to be quite as important, so we would eat crust and all. We also got reconstituted dried milk and eggs to go along with our mutton.

There was a most important Australian representative who lived among the Yank units in the area. His name was Capt. Norman Wilde, and his official business was ANGAU liaison. The initials meant something like Australia, New Guinea Administrative Unit. He knew the whole country: coastline, outback, highlands, jungle, everywhere. He had been stationed in New Guinea for many years and went everywhere in his small plane or by foot. Captain Wilde knew many of the tribes, spoke many of their languages, and acted as a contact person with the natives. Any time he wanted to hitch a ride with one of us he'd just ask and we'd be happy to have him along. He would be up front and give a running narrative of what might be hidden underneath the jungle below. He would scout or suggest possible landing sites that might be okay for C-47s to land or areas that could be used later on as a forward rallying point for fighters or bomber planes as we pushed the Japanese back and needed more advance bases. He chose one site beyond Wau, much closer to Lae, that became a major launch point for the largest paratroop drop in the campaign. The site was called Tsili-Tsili, pronounced "silly silly."

One time Captain Wilde wanted to go into an area that none of us yet knew about, quite a way back in the highlands. He had one Aussie contact person up in that area, but his rare radio contacts were not very informative. The name of the place was Mount Hagen. To the best of the captain's knowledge, the Japanese had not yet made any type of an incursion into the rather large area, either by patrol on foot or by aircraft overfly. The captain wanted to gather some intelligence from the natives, get a new and better radio to his man on the ground, and bring out three or four people. He asked if I would take him there.

This proved to be one of the most interesting trips I made. I've forgotten the mileage, probably between 450 and 500 miles from Port Moresby. That was farther than our fighter cover could go, even with belly tanks. We decided we would be just as well off anyway, because a couple of fighter planes up high might draw some Zeros who were out cruising the intermediate airspace. If interdicted, the fighters wouldn't have enough fuel for much action anyway. We decided to go low along the southern coastline of New Guinea until we arrived at an approximate fall line that the captain would determine. Then we could go inland and approach Mount Hagen from the south.

Captain Wilde wanted to spend as much time on the ground as he could but still get us back to Moresby before dark, so we took off bright and early. I had never been along that coastline, which actually was quite close to Australia. This coast was not at all like the coast on the north shore. Here there were very few villages, a few rivers flowing into the ocean created deltas and swamps, and there were areas with practically no trees or brush. The mountains were off to our right, 20 to 100 miles away. We had no maps. When the captain indicated it was time to turn inland toward Mount Hagen, we started an easy climb as the terrain rose below. About an hour later, we could see a beautiful green valley dead ahead with several signs of habitation. On a nice level spot of ground, the captain pointed and said, "There she is. Let's land." There was a short dirt strip covered with the greenest grass you can imagine. No ruts or tracks in it, because it hadn't been used for some time. Completely surrounding the strip, as a border, was a garden of bright flowers on all four sides. From the air, the scene was peaceful, serene, and beautiful. The view turned out to be the same from the ground.

As we taxied to an area pointed out by Captain Wilde, natives came running toward us from all directions. They kept well away from the airplane, because they had never seen a big bird like this one. They understood machines that flew in the sky because they had seen the smaller planes used earlier by Captain Wilde, but this monster was something else. They jabbered. They pointed at us. They laughed until the captain climbed down the steps and was recognized. They ran to him, shouting and very happy.

These natives were shorter than those we knew. But they were trim, muscular, and generally better-looking than the others. Some of the natives had a jet black skin and were fine-looking people. They gradually came closer to the plane, which we encouraged, and would jabber talk to us and point here and there with quizzical expressions. Obviously they wanted to know more about the plane. Many of them were munching on sugarcane. They would bite off a chunk, chew it a bit, and bend over, laughing in fun. Being with them was a lot like playing with a very small child. They were happy and totally unafraid of us, but still just a bit unsure of the big bird.

We finally got one of their leaders to climb up the stairs. By moving very slowly, we got him a few steps into the cabin. He wouldn't go forward any more without having one of his friends join him. They finally made it to the cockpit, but the trip didn't mean much to them except being able to see their friends outside, at whom they could holler and jabber through the open window. When they started back to the door we stopped them to show them the drop-signal lights. It wasn't too hard to show them that the light colors

The natives came out of the hills for their first sight of the "big birds."

could be changed from green to yellow to red by doing something up in the cockpit, but I don't think they knew how to explain that mystery to those outside. I wanted them to hear the bell-buzzer but didn't turn it on right away. When I tried to indicate by gestures that the bell would be loud and raucous they just didn't comprehend. At first, that is. Finally, after having them hold their hands tightly over their ears, we gave it a try. Just a short buzz sent them about half-crazy. They jumped; they ran to the door; they jabbered louder than ever. Arms and hands flew in all directions. They finally settled down and then, of course, wanted to hear it again and again and again. When they got outside, they explained to the others that they had somehow tamed this wild beast and now any of the lesser folks were free to enter and examine the belly of the bird. Quite a few of them did enter and were very appreciative.

Captain Wilde had gone about his business and said he'd be back about a certain time. He came back about an hour early with two announcements. First, we were to have three additional passengers going back. He had in tow three rather large, frightened Catholic nuns dressed in their worn and tattered habits. He felt they should be moved to safety in case Japanese patrols might locate them. They looked very stern, but they were frightened and uncertain about what was going on. One of them said something including the word "Deutsch." The captain said, "She wants you to know that they are German. She knows the Americans and the Germans are at war, and she does not want to be a burden to you." I took her hand and babbled something in English about being pleased to be able to help get them to safety in Australia. All was well. The nuns smiled.

The captain's second announcement was that the natives insisted that they be able to give us a short version of a "sing-sing." Usually a sing-sing takes a few days, because the natives have to dress and paint up and roast a pig or two in preparation. They also chew betel nuts until they get high. Then they eat sweet potatoes and sing and dance until they drop. They got well on their way in preparing for the feast, until Captain Wilde out of necessity bid them a fond farewell. The nuns climbed aboard. We all waved good-bye, and the natives scattered all over when the engines roared to life. Away we went, missing out on a very exciting time, I'm sure. They were sad to see us leave, and we were really sorry not to be able to stay. They were wonderful and healthy people in a beautiful paradise of peace and color.

Phase III

By mid-1943, the complexion of the war in the South Pacific had changed considerably. While our theater of operations was still playing second fiddle in importance in Washington, delivery of the means to conduct the conflict had improved dramatically. The navy had put into service many new and improved vessels of every conceivable size and description. They were able to deliver men and all kinds of equipment to units in dozens of far-flung areas that badly needed the reinforcements to survive. Men and equipment also went to dozens of positions on scattered beaches and islands, and that made for more extensive ownership by our side throughout the Pacific. Not that the Japanese were not holding on at many of their ill-gotten strongholds; as a matter of fact, they had been able to reinforce some of their larger bases. That's a big old chunk of water out there, and our side just didn't have enough units to acquire and maintain every mile of shoreline along each country or island.

In New Guinea we had several new airfields, especially around the Port Moresby area. In fact, I'd say there were about five major air bases, loosely referred to as Three Mile, Five Mile, Seven Mile, Nine Mile, and Eleven Mile. That referred to the approximate distance from the coast inland to the strip. We had no cross runways. They all ran parallel to the coastline.

We had received an entire new group of troop carriers. Another group was stationed in Australia. The famous Forty-ninth Fighter Group had expanded its power with the addition of new P-40s and a few of the dream fighters, P-38s. Also, a number of heavy long-range bombers showed up. Finally the Americans were beginning to do what the "preliminaries" had been hoping for all along. The Japanese advance was almost stopped. The heavy bombers were softening up targets well behind enemy strongholds, the navy was landing marines on islands large and small, and ground troops were solidifying our holdings in many places.

I once saw a line marking the farthermost advances, in general, of the Japanese forces in the spring of 1943. By the end of 1943, they still held many of those areas along that line, but the Allies (Americans) held quite a few places well behind them. The leapfrog method was apparently going to work out. It was still a long way to Manila and Tokyo, but maybe, just maybe, it was going to work to our advantage.

The Thirty-third Squadron along with the other squadrons of our group, the Sixth and Twenty-first, and the Twenty-second, were still very much in the limelight. They had become the old-timers in the area and of course the ones that knew the country better than anyone else, including MacArthur.

It was about this time that the honorable General "Dug-out Doug" dropped in unannounced on our strip in his B-17. Glotz and I beat it out in our *old* Plymouth to meet him. I think this was his first trip to New Guinea. Glotz and I didn't look too good. Our dress code was not yet in effect. The Plymouth didn't look too good either. We got out to the plane about the time MacArthur climbed down the steps and gave him a real genuine military salute, as we remembered it. We hadn't saluted anyone in a long time.

"Welcome to Ward's, General. What can we do for you?" I asked.

He said, "Is that the best car you have?"

"General, sir," I said, "that's not only the best car we have; it's the only one we know of."

The general's aide dusted off the seat in the car and was able to open the rear door. We loaded in the group of four and they headed out for town. There was a small residence close to the Papua Hotel that became the general's advance office, which he only used about three times. His visit to the scene of action lasted about two hours. When it was over, the Plymouth was just left, without comment, at the end of our strip. He was an arrogant sort, but a great general and soldier. And his clothes were so darned clean they looked out of place. A few weeks later a less raunchy-looking vehicle arrived by boat and was parked near his residence/office. As far as I know, it was never used. The new car was not one of his famous Packards, but it was a lot classier than our Plymouth.

One more story about the Plymouth. We had a couple of good-looking young pilots who somehow had heard about two or three nurses arriving at the nearby tent hospital. It was also rumored that in some cases the medics working that tent hospital might concoct a small potion of medicinal alcohol for barter or whatever. Franni and Glotz got talking about their thirst and the lack of a remedy; they also wanted to verify the rumor about the newly arrived nurses. They gave a thought to taking a jeep toward the hospital and maybe offering to trade a plane ride to any medic that would fix them a libation or introduce them to the nurses. The more they talked, the better the possibilities sounded. A trip to Australia would surely be worth at least a quart and an introduction. And if they were going to go all that distance, they would also plan to have a little visit with the new nurses. Not a bad idea. Maybe they could even take the nurses for a little ride and show them the countryside. But it wouldn't be as apt to work with only a jeep, so why not take the Plymouth four-door town car? Remember, it was a *junker*.

The Plymouth it was. They gassed it up, dusted off the windshield and the front seat, and took off. We who had to stay behind didn't see any more of those two guys until next morning. By the time they woke up, there had been a call or two inquiring, "Who was the three-star general running around the base the previous night?" We didn't know of any heavy rank being around, not even a one-star. But our Plymouth had a license plate holder and in the glove compartment were inserts to fit that holder bearing insignia for each general rank: one, two, three, or four stars. Each had a bright red background with the appropriate number of blue stars. Sure enough. The Plymouth had a three-star plate in the holder. Boys will be boys. They claimed they didn't get to visit with the nurses. They spent the entire evening sipping medicinal alcohol with the medics. And they did put the three-star plate in position, because it was getting late and they didn't want to be stopped at any checkpoints. They had to hurry home to get some sleep so they could fly in the morning. They didn't get stopped. They merely had to salute at each checkpoint. Their comment the next day was that they "don't feel well enough to fly today."

We had the two Schnieders brothers, George and Franni, in our squadron. They were good officers, good pilots, and good friends. There was a third brother (Norbert, maybe, but I'm not sure) who chose to become a naval officer. He became an officer and was captain of a torpedo boat that served in our area (same as John Kennedy). Those torpedo boats were fast! They could probably exceed fifty miles per hour, when pushed, and they performed a lot of hit-and-run missions along the coast. One thing the torpedo guys liked to do was glide slowly, with the engines muffled, along the shoreline just at daybreak to catch a target on the beach. They would give a few bursts from their .50 caliber gun and then roar away, leaving a bunch of scared Japanese wondering what happened. The torpedo guys claimed that on more than one of those fun-type passes they found an early rising Japanese out on the end of the dock doing his mornings, seated in a six- or eight-holer open-air latrine. Can you believe that they actually fired at those guys? They really caught the Japanese with their pants down! I wonder what type of mission symbol they awarded themselves.

As bad luck would have it, on a more serious mission Norbert had his boat shot out from under him. The boat was lost, but the crew was saved. Norbert was told he would have a new torpedo boat just as soon as they could get one to his unit. That was fine with him. He didn't want to go back to the States right away. Instead he looked up George and Franni and came to see them. He'd go along on missions with either one of them, usually flying the copilot seat. For variety he would occasionally fly with one or the other of us. We would always let him do some handling of the plane, and naturally he would like to follow through on takeoffs and landings also. It wasn't too long before George had Norb making takeoffs and landings. Norb really enjoyed the flying, and we all liked him. We were sad to see him get called back to his unit. A few more weeks and we would have had an extra "free" pilot.

We were about to have one of the larger, and more decisive, battles in the area, involving all units of the U.S. forces. It started when a U.S. patrol plane sighted a Japanese convoy leaving Rabaul. After a couple of days, the enemy convoy appeared to be heading for Lae, which is close by Salamaua, Wau, and Bulolo. The Japanese had controlled Lae, Finschhafen, Madang, Wewak, and Hollandia (all major, important facilities), but they obviously could feel the pressure of the U.S. forces and wanted to make a significant show of strength. Whoever controlled Lae completely would have a powerful influence and an area of hundreds of square miles of ocean and land, about like Rabaul.

On the sea, the U.S. Navy gathered ships of all sizes, including some carriers, submarines, and many cruisers and destroyers. They also had a squadron of PT boats. I think this was Norbert Schneiders's PT squadron.

At the U.S.-held positions, heavy and medium bombers began showing up from all directions. I think MacArthur's forces had about three days to set up a trap. And that they did very well. Land bombers occupied every usable strip across the mountains. Support facilities for the U.S. units were way overtaxed. Ever since the Japanese convoy was first sighted, the troop carrier aircraft began hauling fuel in fifty-gallon drums to every strip across the mountains. We'd load up as many barrels as could be stored in the plane, in the cabin, with no bother to tie them down, and head over the hill, where, after landing, we would roll the barrels out at the end of the strip. Then we'd go back for another trip, and another. Sometimes we would make four or five trips in a day—hardly taking time to fuel our own airplanes. When the intercept was to be made, the fighters would want to fuel out of these barrels in order to save time by not having to fly back across the mountains to their home base.

On March 2, 1943, the battle of the Bismarck Sea began. The battle only lasted three days, but all the Japanese transports were sunk. Their escorting destroyers were either sunk or disabled, and their other support vessels were sent hightailing it back home. The victory was very important for our side, a hard loss for the Japanese to accept.

We had just swapped aircraft with a new unit of troop carriers that had arrived in Townsville. It was neat to have nice, new machines at this time, but they sure got dirty and muddy in a hurry. Somehow in the swap we ended up with an extra airplane. Having fourteen planes to work with instead of the thirteen authorized gave the guys in our maintenance and engineering departments a real lift. We wondered how we could have thirteen planes flying almost every day while the other outfits would nearly always have one or more out of service, in need of repair. Our engineering department claimed quite a few records within the group for their efficiency in keeping more aircraft in the air in each monthly report.

Franni and I made a trip to Brisbane to pick up six new pilots and a bit of extra supplies. Some of the mechanical parts had to be acquired from the depot at Cairns. We were going to stay overnight in Brisbane at the officers' quarters at Amberly Field. While getting us to the BOQ, the operations officer asked us if we would like to go out to a very nice home for dinner. We thought that would be great—home cooking. We cleaned up the best we could, and the captain picked us up in a sedan from the motor pool to take us out to the residence. There we found a nice area of town that we had never imagined or been aware of. There was a cluster of large, well-maintained homes. The biggest and grandest house of all was where he turned in.

Must be some kind of a joint, we both thought, *but if so, it is a classy one.* The door was opened by a butler in fine butler uniform who said, "Captain Baxter, please come in." We were not introduced, which made us think more than ever that it was probably a "place." We were ushered into a nice, big den–sitting room, and there Captain Baxter introduced us to our hosts, Mr. and Mrs. So and So. They lived here. This was their home. They were a very gracious and interesting couple from England. He was the representative in Australia for the Bank of England. Probably a rather good job.

Their daughter, who joined us later for an elegant dinner, was evidently a very good friend of Captain Baxter! The English couple just wanted to be kind to him and occasionally to his American friends, no doubt in appreciation of what the Americans were doing to help out the Australians and the British in this horrible time of war. We didn't see many bright lights, but this was one of the most civilized evenings we spent outside of the U.S.A.

We picked up our six new pilots, a crated and heavy B-26 engine, a few other requisitioned items, and 700 pounds of good Australian beer. The weather was lousy and we spent some time on instruments on the way to Cairns. I didn't have any trouble finding the strip and landing in heavy rain, but it was a pretty good storm, so we hurried to get out of there while we could. The field was muddy and soggy, and we surely were overloaded. Visibility was about half the strip, but we figured we'd be in the air by the halfway mark, so we poured on the power. Because the mud held us back, when we were halfway down the strip we still didn't have flying speed. Franni said, "Kick 'er in the ass." Since I always minded him, I did just that. In fact, by the time we were airborne I'd pushed the throttles through the stop wires, where there was a bit of extra power kept in reserve for occasions just like this one. We were on instruments as soon as we left the ground. I throttled back some and headed for Moresby. While climbing through the storm, we got a few little flickers of red warning light on the oil pressure gauge on one engine. But since it wasn't steady, I went ahead and climbed to about 10,000 feet; just in case that one engine decided to quit, we'd have more coasting altitude to use gliding home. Franni and I both knew the plane would fly on one engine for a long way, if necessary, but we were the only ones. We feathered the engine (shut it off and turned the prop to a slicing position into the wind) at 10,000 feet so as not to do any more damage to it than necessary. That, plus the noise the mud made as we took off, had not been too reassuring to those new pilots in the rear. Franni decided to go back and have a little fun with them and maybe scare them some, just as a welcome to New Guinea. He sent one of them up to ride copilot. The new guy sure had a nice, clean uniform on.

One engine was feathered, but I thought it had quite a few good miles left in it. I decided to wait and use it later on in case things got really hairy. I was having a good visit with the new kid copilot while the crew chief kept watching the instruments. The radio operator would stick his head between us for a minute and then head back to his cubbyhole. Franni was telling the guys in the back what would happen if we were going to ditch. He was sure we were not, but better to keep the initiation going some. One of the things he told them was the order in which they would throw things overboard in order to lessen the weight. I later learned what his suggestions, not to be challenged, would be. First would be the miscellaneous equipment and supplies, followed by the B-26 engine, which would take some real heaving. Then the footlockers and bags of the new guys were next. Then they were to tear out radios and other plane equipment that was removable. But the rule was "by gad, don't anyone even suggest we throw out the 700 pounds of beer." When Franni said it might be necessary to push two or three of the passengers out, they got the idea he was just funning them—which he was.

So far, most of the flight had been on instruments and sometimes just a bit turbulent. One time, the radio operator had noticed we were losing 500 feet per minute just from turbulent air. Unbeknownst to me, he reported to Moresby that we had gone down from 10,000 feet to 8,000 feet and were losing altitude at the rate of 500 feet per minute. It wasn't too long before two fighters, who had heard our news about losing altitude, showed up in case we really went in the water. I assured them we were okay, but I didn't mind the company either. Shortly thereafter two C-47s from the Thirty-third showed up. They had been in the air when they heard Ben's report of losing altitude and decided to find us. I accused them of just wanting to watch us go in (which was not my plan). We still had about 1,000 feet altitude when we saw Port Moresby. We cranked up the other engine and landed at home with no problem. We were glad to be on ground, though.

Soon after landing, I got a message that Colonel Imparato wanted to see me. I hustled on over to group headquarters. He gave me hell. His message to me seemed to be, "If you are going to ditch, go ahead and do it. Don't call in and ask for help and disrupt everything up here." That was the first I knew that Ben had been a bit overexcited when he called in about losing altitude while on single-engine. I apologized for ruining the colonel's day and decided he just didn't like me. Later on, when I came back to the States and was up for assignment, there was a message from Imparato asking me to come work with him in a nice, cushy job. I didn't take the job, but I gathered all was forgiven even though I failed to ditch when we were supposed to.

When I try to recall the last half of 1943, it seems like during this time we weren't quite as busy as before. But referring again to my Form 5, which certainly didn't record every flight, the workload must have been about the same. For June of '43 I show twenty-eight combat missions. I guess we were just getting more and more acquainted with our immediate area, because other research shows that the strips farther up the coast and even Salamaua, Lae, and Nadzab still belonged to the Japanese.

There were quite a few new bombers, both medium and heavy, and they were softening up a number of spots that MacArthur had his eye on and wanted for himself. New and better fighter planes, especially the P-38s, made things more secure for us and also for the heavy bombers when they stayed within range of their escort. All the fighters were using belly tanks for extra fuel, which, of course, made extra range possible. The P-38s carried two outside wing tanks, which they would use outbound and then jettison when the fight started. Imagine up to sixty or eighty fighters upstairs, each with two tanks about eight feet long, all being dropped at almost the same time. Must have looked like the sky was falling to those guys on the ground. I don't think the Japanese were using auxiliary fuel tanks on their planes at this stage.

Dick Bong was one of those great P-38 pilots and already an American hero for his accomplishments in aerial combat. He was wild in the air. He was a super expert pilot. Those Zero pilots he didn't knock down he must have scared the "bejimminy" out of. His wingman was a Montana hero named Stanley "Bud" Johnson. The wingman is the second guy in a two-plane element, whose job it is to see that the lead guy doesn't get shot and can spend his time maneuvering and aiming and firing. They made a perfect team and flew as a pair for many missions until Bud was lost in a huge scrap over Rabaul in autumn of 1943.

In July, I recorded twenty combat missions, plus one four-day trip to Townsville, Brisbane, Sydney, and Darwin, which took twenty flying hours. In August, I flew twenty-seven combat missions, plus twenty flying hours hauling dignitaries around. We were still busy.

A couple of the changes that were taking place included the more frequent arrivals of rather high-ranking officers, but not quite high enough to have their own plane, who wanted to see what their subordinates were doing. Of course, if their picture got taken while they were dressed in combat gear so much the better. Rightly or wrongly, I give credit to George Schneiders for naming our occasional hitchhiker going into the combat zone. If he wore only one star, the visitor was called "the lowest form of general." Without their insignia on and put into the airplane with a bunch of barrels of gas, they didn't appear too intimidating.

We also started hearing our first broadcasts from Tokyo Rose. She would play good jazz music, which we enjoyed, and tell us how well the Imperial Japanese forces were doing in the war. These remarks were only partially true. She also reported on the hard times in the U.S. mainland. I guess the lines for cigarettes were long. She also gave many suggestions that we quit the war and go home to those families who wanted us. I didn't see anyone who took that propaganda to heart. Lack of morale was not a problem for us. Then there were the Indian talkers. Mostly Navajo, I guess. Our Signal Corps people, mostly navy, had broken most of the enemy codes, and the Japanese had broken some U.S. codes. But when the Indian talkers came on the radio, the Japanese went bonkers. The talkers were used a lot in important battle situations. The Japanese never had a clue as to what sort of jabber that was, going "open" over the airwaves. I never did hear the Indian talkers. I wish I had.

The Markham River runs from the northern side of the highlands of Papua downward through a long, wide valley and empties into the ocean at Lae. There were very few villages along the valley floor, as the natives prefer hillsides for growing their sweet potatoes and trees and jungle for protection from other warriorlike native tribes. There were no roads, a few footpaths, some *kunai* grass up to five or six feet tall, and plenty of space. I can imagine Generals MacArthur and Kenney saying, "Aha" (if that's the way they talked when together), "take a look at this spot as a potential for a great big U.S. air base. We can have as many runways as we want and for as long as we want. And when we capture Lae, we will for the first time have good access to the Bismarck Sea. Lae is only thirty-five miles away. How do we go about it?"

I'm sure General Kenney responded about like this: "This should not be a piecemeal operation. I say we go balls-out, hit it with everything we have. I think I know just how to do it. We'll give Lae a bomb softening up like hasn't been seen in this area yet. The Jap air base will be reduced to a minor facility so they won't be able to mount much of a counterattack when we move into this area, here." Then he would point at the map, saying, "We will do a big paratroop drop right here at Nadzab. I have available, somewhere, 1,500 paratroopers, the 503d Parachute Infantry Regiment, and eighty-six troop carrier airplanes to drop them."

"Sounds good to me," says MacArthur. "Let's do it in September."

So by the end of August 1943 the paratroopers were assembled at a new airstrip called Tsili-Tsili; two new troop carrier groups of C-47 aircraft were ready to drop them. Drop day was set for September 5.

The Thirty-third was not invited to be present. Too old and worn out, I suppose.

It was a beautiful operation. I still have a single photo, about ten by twenty inches, which shows all of this:

1. A low-level smoke screen laid down by two B-25s, one along the base leg along the hills and one at ninety degrees along the approach leg over the river and the landing zone.
2. The first wave of paratroopers hitting the ground jumping from about twelve C-47s. (The planes are also in the picture.)
3. About twelve more C-47s on the approach, some with their troopers in the air and some just ready to unload.
4. More C-47s are on the base leg. There are more yet to come.
5. Overhead at about 5,000 feet are ten P-38s in two plane elements, acting as close cover. I'm sure more fighter aircraft are on location, much higher and outside the drop zone perimeter, but not in the photo.
6. Then over on the right-hand side is a single B-17 carrying either MacArthur or Kenney or both, watching the show. This is a fantastic photo shot by some official photographer.

There was practically no enemy opposition on the ground or in the air. As is often said, "A sizable show of force is a real deterrent to a timid enemy."

As far as I know, the only use of the Thirty-third in this operation was to have two of us bring in a Caterpillar dozer, half in each plane. I was pilot on one plane and had the Cat tracks and frame and about ten guys to get it out the door once we landed. The pilot of the other plane had the engine, seat, and controls and also a few men to manhandle it out the door. We landed after the troopers had set out four red flags indicating four corners of a place that looked okay to land. That was less than an hour after the first paratrooper jumped. We had some rations, a helmet, our side arms, and a few bullets just in case we had to stay on the ground. We didn't much care for that. I said, "I bet we can get off from here as easy as we got in, so let's give 'er a try." We raised a lot of dust but got airborne and headed for Tsili-Tsili. Within three hours, dozens of troop carriers started hauling in Aussie infantry and tons and tons of supplies.

Nadzab became a large, important air base and staging area that was a significant factor in the march to the Philippines. I flew over Nadzab in 1976. It was a ghost airport, only a few native huts around. But Lae, where I looked around on the ground, was a bustling, cosmopolitan, clean city of several thousand people and with an active harbor. Most of the natives even wore clothes.

The sparse records I have that show exactly what the Thirty-third was doing day by day during the latter part of 1943 don't indicate many specific things that occurred. I know we flew almost every day, probably to quite a few new landing strips as well as the old ones. As the perimeters of U.S. positions were gradually expanded, we just had more funny little places to haul "items in need," as well as to the newly established bases like Nadzab, Goodenough Island, and Finschhafen.

By now I was CO of the Thirty-third, but I didn't issue a whole lot of orders. I inherited a first sergeant who was almost a law unto himself. Since I didn't know much about military paper procedures and neither did he, we sometimes failed to see eye to eye. Occasionally I prevailed.

A few weeks earlier, Colonel Carter had issued a written order making me CO of the Twenty-second Squadron. Carter was Group

Commander. Somehow I received a copy of that order. I grabbed a jeep and headed over to the 374th group headquarters, about three miles away. I found the colonel out on the flight line and said, "Hey, Colonel, I don't want this. Not the Twenty-second! Not those guys."

"Gosh," he replied, or maybe it was something stronger, "I thought you would like that. Got any suggestions who might make a good CO for them?"

I hadn't given it any thought but responded in a hurry. "Sure. Watson would be just right. He is big and he is tough. He could shape the Twenty-second up better than anyone."

The Colonel seemed to think that would be okay, and he promised to send over a cancellation to me tomorrow.

The next day, my one-day tour as CO of the Twenty-second ended. The same order named Watson their new CO. Watson was very pleased.

Very shortly thereafter I received a written order from Carter making me CO of the Thirty-third. He hadn't mentioned it to me, nor had I asked, but I guess he knew that was what I wanted. I have to believe the guys in the Thirty-third liked it also. But I still didn't have any written orders sending me overseas.

Remember the U.S. Thirty-second and Forty-first infantry divisions? They were sloshing over a much broader area of the north side of New Guinea pointed toward the Philippines. They were doing a dirty job but doing it well. We were still the suppliers of most of their requirements, but they did receive some heavier equipment, some larger trucks and even a few small tanks, by sea. They sure had a hard time trying to find places to use those tanks. Most of their supplies were moved from the landing fields by native carriers over paths and trails through the jungles. The natives were very loyal to our side.

We lost another one of our original thirteen crews on May 12, 1943. Walter Thompson and Ranges were the pilots, and the three-man crew were Cheek, Loy, and Wolfberger. That brings the bad totals to twenty-one men and six aircraft lost in six and a half months, from the original thirteen planes.

I have no idea how many heavy bombers were lost by this time. There were quite a few, because they were going on long flights without fighter escort. Because they had ten- or twelve-man crews, their casualty numbers were high. The fighter pilots were still doing quite well, because they were so much more skilled than the Japanese pilots they encountered. My personal, unofficial opinion is that the U.S. fighter pilots had a victory ratio of about ten to one.

Occasional U.S. bomber attacks had been made on Rabaul, but not in force until October 1943. On one day, 349 planes, including a large escort of P-38s, attacked Rabaul. This was the first time that the P-38s were able to fly cover that far into enemy territory. That was because we had finally gotten enough fuel supply on hand across the mountains at their refueling base, so the P-38s could take off from Port Moresby, top off by hand pump out of barrels at those strips, catch up with the bombers just as they reached the Rabaul areas, drop their belly tanks, fend off the Zeros for fifteen minutes, and just have enough fuel and fumes to get back to Dobo or Popondetta. They would hand-pump enough fuel to then take them back across the mountain. This air raid did monumental damage to the entire Japanese facility, but I'm sure a high price was paid by our airmen.

More frequent follow-up raids were made, but in smaller numbers, as men and equipment became available. Early in November, another large raid with 160 planes, heavy bombers escorted by P-38s, took place. However, this time the Japanese had a lot of additional Zeros available for combat. That, plus bad weather, proved very costly to us. Our side lost twenty planes.

It was on this particular raid that Bud Johnson was lost. He was a P-38 pilot from Lewistown, Montana, and the husband of the former Barbara Wilson. (She was the gal that someone had invited to go up around Charlo to hunt pheasants, the co-ed who couldn't fix her zipper and was sent to see if Mrs. Wamsley couldn't help fix it. Barbara has always said the Wamsleys must be okay to have parents like those two in Charlo.) As a combat veteran, Bud had become a fighter ace in the Ninth Squadron of the Forty-ninth Fighter Group at Moresby. They were the guys we low-flying troop carriers loved to see overhead flying cover for us as we did our bit down below. Those fellows and their machines were the very best.

Dick Bong had become the leading fighter ace in the theater, later in the entire history of the air force; he ultimately shot down about forty enemy planes. He and Bud teamed up as a pair, with Bong flying leadman and Bud flying wingman. On this November day they got to Rabaul in bad weather, just in time to help protect the bombers. The Japanese countered with everything they had. There were lots of new Zeros, antiaircraft fire, and even some old Bettys. The Japanese were making a last-ditch stand to save Rabaul. Our guys were proving to them that Rabaul was doomed. It had been the major sea and air base in that part of the Pacific for the Japanese since hostilities began in the South Pacific, and this series of raids was the calling card by the U.S. Air Force that all of New Britain was about to be reclaimed.

Reports from returning pilots told of that raid being one big, wild scrap with things happening so fast no one could see the entire picture. Besides, the planes were in and out of clouds every few seconds. The P-38s had only a few minutes of fighting time because of fuel consideration. That gave the heavy bombers time to drop their loads, head into cloud cover, and then head for home. The bombing mission was totally successful, except for the planes lost. As the P-38s held back in order to cover the heavies for the final few minutes, Bud's element was hit by several Zeros. A wild dogfight left planes scattered. Bong headed toward home as a P-38 came up and took wing-man position on him. It was not Bud. Several P-38s failed to return to the refueling base. Because of the battle circumstances, no one of the returning pilots could definitely establish whether they had been over land or water. If the missing pilots had bailed out over water they could well have been picked up by the Japanese. There was no evidence that any had. On the other hand, if they bailed out over land or survived a crash landing they would most likely be picked up by natives and hidden from the Japanese. There were instances of that happening over and over in this area. In some cases it was months before the natives got a downed airman to a "coast watcher," where contact with the Allies would be made; then the airman could be picked up by a PBY flying boat or by submarine.

By the time Dick Bong got back to his base, he had orders sending him to the States forthwith. Any more word on Bud was inconclusive, but Bong had the feeling that he would be okay. All fighter pilots feel that way, fortunately. There were probably several reasons to get Dick back to the States pronto. One, of course, was to protect the air force's ace of aces, at least for a time. Another was to show him off to the public because, as a genuine hero, he could help sell war bonds. His hometown of Superior, Wisconsin, also wanted him at a dedication of their new municipal airport, which, naturally, they named after him. This was in the fall of 1943.

Barbara Wilson Johnson's sister, Joan, lived in Superior, Wisconsin. When Barbara received official word that Bud was MIA, she and her mother went to Superior to stay with Joan while Joan was having her baby. A day or two after their arrival, the daily newspaper told of the upcoming dedication of the airport and that Dick Bong was in town. Barbara called Bong's mother and told her who and where she was. Dick showed up and spent the afternoon with her. He still thought there was a chance that Bud would be rescued. But that was not to be.

In the 1960s at Malmstrom Air Force Base in Great Falls, Montana, a full-fledged military ceremony and dedication was held to honor Bud. The electronic control center for the entire Minute-Man-missile program was at this facility, and this program was probably the greatest deterrent force in existence at that time. The control center was called Stanley Johnson Memorial Hall.

While my wife, Barbara, and I were visiting my sister, Marney, at her lake place in northern Wisconsin in 1989, we three decided to drive up to Duluth, Minnesota. To get there we passed through Superior, Wisconsin. Marney was driving, I was riding shotgun, and Barbara was in the backseat. As we entered Superior there was a nice sign reading: RICHARD BONG AIRPORT. Marney, being a reputable tour guide, pointed out the sign and told us what a fine airport it was. She did know that the airport namesake was a pilot in the South Pacific, so she asked if I knew anything about him or had heard of him. I said I'd heard a lot about him. In fact, he had flown fighter cover for me and my squadron in New Guinea frequently. And by the way, he and Barbara were friends.

Barbara then told her story of the coincidence of being in the same town at dedication time of the Richard Bong Airport. Forty-eight years after the fact it seemed a most unusual story.

Now back to our story in New Guinea in the winter of 1943. By the end of that year we somehow got some living quarters with wood floors. Probably the lumber from the old ex–374 group headquarters. I was made base commander of Ward's Airdrome. I was still commanding officer of the Thirty-third Squadron.

On Christmas Eve, 1943, a traveling Catholic priest came by. Several of us grabbed our helmets and stood in the mud, happily listening to a Christmas service. I don't remember it, but my Form 5 says I flew two combat missions that day and also two on Christmas Day.

Phase IV

In February of 1944, we had lost John Donovan and his crew on a flight from Townsville, Australia, to Goodenough Island, which is across New Guinea and about 100 miles beyond the northern New Guinea coastline. The other crew members were Zimmerman, Mosely, and Polson. None of those were among the crew members on the original flight over, but all had been with us for several months. Donovan came to our squadron because he was a friend of the Schnieders boys from Loyola Marymount University and asked to be assigned to the Thirty-third when he arrived in Australia as an unassigned pilot.

On his flight from Townsville, Donovan's destination was certainly within the area of potential enemy air attack, but unofficially we decided his disappearance was more likely to have been caused by weather. I remember the day very well. The weather was not good for flying. The day before, I had made a similar trip to Milne Bay and had seen three waterspouts while coming back across the water. A waterspout is a tornado over water that is sucking up water from the ocean. Pilots give them a wide berth when they see them because they are solid as rocks and have vicious winds nearby. Other pilots that were flying that day saw two spouts, widely separated, but the weather conditions were still extreme. The time that we decided Donovan was really lost was uncertain, because we had no communication with his destination. Donovan's disappearance was probably reported by a pilot on the same mission when Donovan's plane failed to arrive at Goodenough.

Since Donovan was a very special friend of mine and I was the squadron boss and also about one-fourth macho, I announced I'd head out at first light on a search mission. There was a bigger boss guy around who said there would be no flying until the weather abated: "The airport is closed." He did tell me there was an Aussie outfit nearby and they had a flying boat, a seaplane, and suggested maybe they would do a search. They would. The next morning bright and early I became a copilot to the only pilot they had that knew how to fly that seaplane, which was a three-engine Dornier Flying Boat. It had no wheels, and the instruments were labeled with German language labels designating what they were. We took along his "batman" as a pair of eyes and also to untie and tie the machine to a dock, if need be.

Despite the sad circumstances, the flight was a memorable experience. The plane was so old that the engines rattled, and it was very slow-moving. It had a long range, if you could read the fuel gauges, and apparently the hull didn't leak. The Dornier was a lot like a Ford trimotor with a hull instead of landing gear. Because of bad weather, we couldn't see water for a long way out, so concentrated the search nearer the New Guinea coastline, from about opposite Port Moresby, around the end of New Guinea, out from Milne Bay, and then up the other side to Goodenough. I guess we covered a lot of square miles of ocean by zigzagging from shoreline to maybe 200 miles offshore. When the weather closed in, we would just locate another area of water visibility. I think we always had at least one raft aboard our C-47s, so we were looking for a raft while over water. The search was futile but seemed worth the effort. Remember Rickenbacker? He spent almost thirty days in a raft before being rescued.

We spent the night in Milne Bay and then repeated the reverse search the following day. The pilot let me do a landing in a nice, smooth bay. The good part of that was the long runway. Because your rear end is about water level, it is hard to make the plane contact the water. You have a tendency to scrunch upward. The good part is that if you will just let the speed decrease and the plane settle down, sooner or later you will be floating in the water. The touchdown sounds awful, too. Noisy.

There is an entry in my Form 5 showing that we were in that Dornier for twenty-seven hours, but I doubt that. Maybe two days at ten hours each. No trace of Donovan was ever found.

The Sixth, Twenty-second, and Thirty-third squadrons spent a short period of time assigned to Townsville, which I considered an improvement. We had regular barracks, a respectable mess hall, indoor toilets, and much improved flying conditions. Australia is a large country, about the same size as the U.S.A. The northern part of the country was still not totally secure from Japanese invasion; thus a lot of our trips were up to that part of the country. Our air force had a couple of heavy bombardment bases up there by now and also one or two fighter units. Darwin was well protected, but since frequent bomber raids originated there, it was also a fair-game target for the enemy. The Japanese had not yet totally given up the idea of owning Darwin. After all, they were still trying to establish and resupply bases in Dutch New Guinea, Sumatra, Java, and other parts of Malaysia. Since Australia was settled only around the coastline, our trips were longer and a bit less stressful, unless we got lost over the vast outback. This area was not an official combat zone.

I recall one trip that ended up taking us almost all around the border of the country. It was a night flight from Brisbane to Fenton. We got there too early, and the base didn't seem to want to light up a runway so we could land. We were in contact with them and knew we were close, but a night as black as pitch and no lights of any kind made it just a bit eerie. Even at first light the landing strips were so well camouflaged we went right by them without knowing it. A few miles away, practically inside Darwin city limits, was another U.S. base, and they were lighted up like a carnival. Here the tower operators told us how to locate Fenton. By the time we got back to Fenton, the coffee was on and they were happy to unload some much needed supplies.

The next stop on this particular odyssey was Broome. On the map Broome appeared to be a town of some size, but it was no more than a good-sized village by U.S. standards. I doubt if I ever knew just what supplies we picked up there, but it was something important that had to get to Potshot. We had never heard of Potshot, nor could we locate the place on any map.

Someone was able to give us a contact method with Potshot by radio and a brief description of how we would find the place to land. When we got to the general location and found the bay as described, it was a welcome and reassuring sight. The bay was about half the size of San Francisco Bay. The flight had been about like flying from Seattle to San Francisco at 2,000 feet and never seeing any live thing on either land or water. The only visible traffic in the bay was a small freighter and a couple of barges hauling their cargo to shore. It turned out there were two or more U.S. submarines in port that were so well camouflaged they could not be seen from the air. Potshot was a small but complete facility for resupply of a squadron of our underwater craft that roamed the Indian Ocean. This base wasn't exactly a first-class location for the kind of R & R the submariners would have liked, but it was better than being underwater for another sixty days. There was no town and very few roads. For living quarters ashore, those navy guys had deluxe tents, electricity, a gymnasium, and a first-class mess hall. We stayed overnight and were treated to a fine meal, bunks with springs and sheets, good showers, and a movie. The main thing I recall is the breakfast. They had good coffee, canned peaches, ham, and powdered eggs. For dessert there was a pan about eighteen inches square of good ole pork 'n' beans set on each table. That pan was at least three inches deep. Those guys went after those beans like a bear takes after honey. I guess they don't get to have many beans aboard a submarine—close quarters, you know, and you can't trust anyone. The morale of those submariners at Potshot was perfect, very high. I was glad they were on our side.

We hauled mail, guys going on leave, and a high-ranking courier on the next leg to Perth. On this particular flight, I think Shea was flying copilot. I know I was pilot when we located the Aussie base where we were to land. No trouble with the radio instructions, no trouble with air traffic, but after a long, boring flight, Shea had to do something. As we passed over the field and the tower told us we were next to land, Shea hollered, "Forced landing!" and pulled the throttles all the way back. That wasn't uncommon among friendly pilots. Just sort of a game of chicken that we sometimes tested our best friends with.

The idea was to *not* do a normal landing procedure: no downwind leg, no base leg, no mile or two of approach, no jockeying for more or less throttle so you could get a nice, straight approach to touchdown. In this game you *don't* use the throttles except in a critical situation. Instead, you plan a circle, lose your altitude, ask for the gear down, and end up coming over the fence with just a few feet to spare and then touch down just as you straighten out with the runway, without having touched the throttles. If you had to have more throttle to reach the runway, you lost the game. If you didn't land right on the end of the runway and floated down the field, you also lost. I kinda hate to admit it, but I swear I landed on the first ten feet of runway. Probably just as well that Shea is gone, because he can't verify this. But if it had been Carlson that was with me, I suppose he would claim that he was the one who landed the plane and I played "forced landing." It's easier to tell stories when the other guy is not present.

As we continued the flight, we realized that across the bottom side of Australia there is a lot of nothing. We had a fuel stop at an Aussie air base about halfway between Perth and Adelaide. The country was like what we now see on television—nothing. The balance of the circle trip was routine: overnight at Melbourne, Sydney, and on to Townsville. Lots of instrument time.

By now there had been a few people sent back to the States. The selection was made according to rather mysterious qualifications. Most of the personnel returning to the States appeared to have been those who had originally come down from the Philippines or those sent to Australia unassigned and had arrived before the original air echelons arrived. I had made a few requests to group headquarters to send some of our unit members back home, but none had been so ordered. There was no authorized system under which to make that request, but if some person, officer or enlisted man, appeared to be getting a little batty, I'd have the first sergeant draft a polite request for the man's return to the States. No soap. And we got no help from the big shots at group to tell us how to get a rotation program going.

Our flight surgeon and I had a few visits about alternative plans, but none of them seemed to work. We ultimately decided we

157

hadn't been forceful enough. We decided to trump up a disaster case. "Let's send something through the channels about a complete nut and see what happens," Doc said. He said he would write up a medical report no one could refuse. We drafted up two or three pages of a real tear-jerker situation. I verified his conclusions, and he verified my summary of the hardships and accomplishments of this person and his need for immediate medical treatment in the States. Family hardships were added to the report, just to fill out an extra page of reasons to expedite the rotation.

When we finished this model proposal it was so sad we almost cried—or maybe we could get the military police to restrain this "case" until departure orders were received. So far we hadn't selected a person to test this new procedure. I suggested someone. Since we hadn't put him on any of the prior requests, he had never been turned down. I got someone else to type up this beautiful piece of flimflam. Doc and I signed each page and dispatched it over to group. We presumed it would be put in the waste basket like all the previous requests. But we hoped that sometime soon someone in authority would consider our worthy request and act on it, request additional information, or at least turn it down officially.

The very next day came an envelope with orders:

[Capt. ———, OXO [serial numbers], effective this date is hereby relieved under provisions of . . . , will report . . . , by best available military transportation . . . , to such and such a military installation [close to his official home address] . . . , with per diem . . . , and after 30 days delay en route . . . , will report to such and such base as to be determined by . . . [someone, someplace, somehow].

Boy, this was a breakthrough. So far I hadn't mentioned anything about this to our lucky pilot. I got to him at once and told him to pack up and ship out. He was very pleased. It didn't take him long to get ready, and it didn't take long to organize a farewell party for our first repatriate. We were in Townsville, you know, so there was lots of beer, food, and other guys to celebrate. There was lots of good spirit, backslapping, speculation, "do you remembers," and just general conviviality.

All of the official papers had been gathered from somewhere and delivered to our "victim." He was free to go. Included in those papers was a copy of his 201 file, which is an officer's complete record of military service. Normally that file is not given to an officer until he separates from the service, but somehow it was copied and placed in his transfer document file. In the middle of the farewell festivities he came up beside me and asked if I would come on over to his bunk area for a minute. When we got there, he sat on the bunk, looking just a bit sad I thought, and got out his 201 file. He rummaged through it a bit and came out with a copy of the request that the doc and I had conjured up to forward on to group. He asked, "Am I as crazy as this thing says?"

There was no one in our outfit as uncrazy at that time, but I hadn't explained our strategy to him before he read the bad medical evaluation in his packet. He was sure relieved when I assured him it was just an exaggerated analysis of a potential situation that we hoped to use in the days following to get some of our most worthy guys back Stateside. He knew, as did most of the pilots, that several unsuccessful attempts had been made to get a rotation program working. Over the next few months that plan was used with some success to send our old pilots home.

For the pilots who remained, there was quite a bit of military action up the north coast of New Guinea, as well as the islands immediately offshore. The names of some of those newly acquired locations were unique. I didn't fly into all of them, but in retrospect the military activity showed that the war was moving onward. By mid-1944, instead of just a few troop carrier aircraft, as was the case in 1942, there was a whole bunch of C-47s operating out of various command headquarters to those many bases. Some of the bases were named: Saider, Madang, Wewak, Dagua, Aitape, Wakde, Biak, Boram, But, Gussap, Dumps, Owi, Tadji, and, of course, Finschhafen. In checking some newly acquired reference material, I see that our group, which consisted of the Sixth, Twenty-first, Twenty-second, and Thirty-third squadrons, was sent to Townsville in June 1944 as a permanent change of station. It took sixteen squadrons in New Guinea to replace our four. Maybe there was a little more work to be done over a greater area than we had been handling.

We were in Townsville for less than three weeks when we were told that one of our squadrons was needed back in New Guinea. By July 3, the permanent change of station was reversed for that squadron. So much for the barracks and food of the mainland for one of our squadrons. The four squadron commanders were called in and told of this development. I was invited to draw a slip out of a cap to see which unit went back to the jungles away from civilization. I recall my exact words: "There is no point in me drawing. I'd be sure to draw Thirty-third." Since none of the other guys wanted to draw either, I drew. Sure enough, it said: "Thirty-third." We would be going back to Ward's Airdrome. Take your time. Load up tonight and get there tomorrow! It was already after supper. Another bit of verbal order sifted through: "Send part of your radio section up to Finschhafen." *Finschhafen? Good Gawd, no, not there.* That was the point of the Huon peninsula that the Japanese and the Aussies had been trading back and forth. For over a year there had been minor skirmishes over a small piece of swamp that nobody should want. Finschhafen had a small landing strip made out of the metal grids we had hauled in long ago, only a few jeeps, no electricity, mud two feet deep, mosquitoes, rain every day, and rain every night. That's all it had going for it. Not a fit place. But it did set up the scenario for the "Great Generator Heist."

It was a dark night. There was a lot of grumbling as the guys loaded up all of our possessions. Word got out that in addition to being back at Port Moresby, we might have a secondary base at Finsch. Having a secondary base usually meant we'd all be going there before too long. And it was a hellhole. There would be no electricity. The mosquitoes would eat you alive. But word also got out that there was a gas-powered electric generator over at a supply depot not very far from where the planes were being loaded in Townsville. Seemed natural for a couple of guys to reconnoiter the area of the depot by jeep. So they did. I was not one of them. The leader, a pilot, decided on a plan. He got a good-sized crash truck with a boom hoist and hook, a driver, and about six husky guys and headed toward the depot front gate with all lights on. They were making lots of noise, going fast enough to indicate hurry, and slid the truck to a stop almost on top of the armed guard.

"Hey, Soldier, I've gotta get a generator outta here and we ain't got no time. The captain will be along in a minute with the requisition. You know where the generator is?"

Well, he didn't know for sure, but he'd check the inventory and see if they had one and where it might be located in the depot. Our guys knew where it was, right up against the fence about sixty yards from the front gate. The crew leader yelled out like he meant for the guard to hear so he wouldn't shoot, "I see it right down here! Yup, it's a big one! That's the one we are supposed to get! Back that truck along the fence, and we'll just lift it over!" The guard continued checking the inventory. The truck reached the proper position. Someone knew how to work the hoist. A couple of guys stepped in the hook, hung onto the cable, and were lifted over the fence in nothing flat. They fastened some lift hooks on the crate and hollered, "Take 'er up!" That big crate was lifted up over the fence with the two guys on top of it, placed gently down on the flatbed, and unhooked. The crew headed out with the prize aboard. As they went by the gate house, the leader hollered to the guard, "Thanks for your help!" The guard didn't shoot.

I guess the men had a helluva time getting that crate through a cargo door into one of our planes. But they did. And they didn't wait till morning to take off. By morning, they were halfway to New Guinea. I understand it was a beautiful piece of American equipment, unused, the only one of its kind in the country, and, by golly,

161

it was going to provide electricity to our guys and to the Aussies in exchange for food and other treasures at Finschhafen.

Nothing much came of the squadron's "move" to Finschhafen. We didn't send a radio contingent up there as we had expected to do. We sent in an occasional flight but didn't move there. The Japanese and the Aussies kinda quit fighting for possession, and the place became just a spot on the map. Nobody wanted it. Perhaps whoever got the generator was declared winner.

A sequel: The members of the Thirty-third had been holding biannual reunions since the mid-1960s when I attended my first one in Seattle, in 1982. They were still talking about the "Great Generator Heist" after thirty-eight years. I got four different versions of the conditions of the event and of the personnel involved—and each one telling me about it was absolutely sure his version was correct. One even claimed he was one of the guys who went over the fence to hook the line to the crate and that I was the guy who hoodwinked the guard. Not so. But this incident does make one realize that events of long ago do seem real in more versions than in a single, accurate telling. I enjoy hearing about the tales of events that are told at every reunion. The above story is one of those known as a "Midnight Requisition."

Remembering my experience in Australia, several significant facts come to mind: Do you know about the rabbit fence in Australia? Way back in the 1920s or 1930s a proliferation of jackrabbits in the huge outback of western Australia was worrisome enough to the citizens of the higher class, the eastern coastline, that they formed a commission to find out how to keep the rabbits from working their way to the east coast. They couldn't hunt them all. They couldn't drown them all because of lack of water. They decided the only way to keep them out was to fence them in. So they built a rabbitproof fence from the extreme north of the country to the southern coast. That's a long way, just about the same distance as from International Falls, Minnesota, to Houston, Texas. They built this rabbitproof fence all that distance, in a straight line, to hold the rabbits on the west side. And the Aussies claim it worked. No wild rabbits on one side and a bunch on the other side. From the air the fence was quite visible, the longest fence in a straight line anyone had ever seen. The Aussies had another straight line record, a transcontinental railroad across the southern states from Adelaide to Perth with a portion almost 800 miles long without a curve. A dubious record.

We took a bit of the curse off the forced return to New Guinea by establishing a source of rations a whole lot better than those provided by the quartermaster. Occasionally, maybe once a month, one of our planes would make a food run to Alice Springs, far from any military action, almost in the center of Australia. Whoever volunteered for the run would gather up a bunch of cash—I think pretty much from the officers, as we had no way to spend anything and could contribute freely—and head out. They would refuel at Cairns and go on to Alice Springs, where they would buy a bunch of fresh beef, vegetables, eggs, and beer. Then it was refuel, fly on to Cairns to refuel, and then home to Port Moresby. The officers and the enlisted men had separate mess by now, so the fresh goodies would be split fifty-fifty. We and quite a few guests would eat well for a few days. Thank you, taxpayers, for all that fuel. We appreciated it.

Meanwhile, the front line of the heavy war zone was gradually moving forward and onward even though in some areas the Japanese were still reinforcing miscellaneous positions that had long been bypassed by the United States. This territory included the bottom of the line, Bougainville (next to Guadalcanal) and New Britain, which was still a threat to Port Moresby and its area of control. The leapfrog program of the U.S. commanders did leave a few hot spots in the islands.

While not common knowledge until after the fact, the entire 374th Group of Troop Carriers, including the Thirty-third was scheduled to move to Hollandia, if and after it was taken away from the Japanese. They had 11,000 troops there. Eleven thousand.

General Adachi was their boss. Not many miles away, on Biak Island, was Colonel Kuzume with 11,000 more troops. Like the wounded cowboy said while lying on the barroom floor after a fight, "Where'd all those guys come from?"

The U.S. troops expected to dislodge those 22,000 Japanese were the U.S. I Corps, commanded by the famous General Eichelberger. But guess who was to spearhead that action: the Forty-first Division, at both locations, Hollandia and Biak. Remember those guys? The Forty-first was made up of National Guard units principally from Montana, Minnesota, Wisconsin, and Michigan that we had hauled over the hill from Moresby to Dobodura and Buna way back in the fall of 1942. Here they were, almost 2,000 miles up the coast, a lot of it done by foot, and expected to take on both of these targets "because of their experience and dependability." General Fuller was their CO. The battles were going to take some time.

My office at Ward's was quite elegant: two rooms, no interior walls, wood flooring, screened exterior walls, a thatched roof, and a screen door. It had been occupied by a high mucky muck who had moved on. Also, I had my own jeep. After all, I was a major at the time. But Mermelstein often let me know he ran our show anyway. I was squadron CO, base CO, and a member of General MacArthur's ADVON staff. I never did wholly understand what that last one was, but supposedly it was an advanced echelon board to advise the general. The CO of ADVON was Gen. Ennis Whitehead, Mac's chief of staff. He was a good guy. I don't recall any specific meetings, only an occasional contact about some minor subject. The sad part was that I wasn't able to give MacArthur any advice. Ennis did all the advising from his office adjoining the big general's down in Brisbane. I once asked an infantry captain if he had any suggestions I could pass on regarding the conduct of the conflict. To quote, "Tell that fuckin' general to take this goddamned war and shove it up his ass." I guess I caught the captain on a bad day.

It was a year and a half after George Vandevort and his plane loaded with infantrymen disappeared (November 10, 1942) when an Aussie officer from their search and rescue unit came into my office unannounced. He had a small package that contained several scraps of paper and material that had just been recovered from the recently discovered wreck of Vandevort's *Flying Dutchman* on a remote mountainside of the Owen Stanleys. Some natives had discovered the wreck earlier and finally reported the location to the Australians. Vandevort had been a close friend of mine. Because of our alphabetical inferiority (V and W) we had stood side by side in many a formation during our cadet training.

The Aussie was able to verify that it was Vandevort's plane and that the twenty or twenty-two infantrymen had been killed; about half were killed in the crash, and the rest died later. One of the crew members, Kirschner, successfully walked out to civilization, but at least three others well enough to try walking out were never heard from again. The walk out took Kirschner nearly forty days. At the time of the incident, we had searched from the air for weeks and weeks for this crash site without any clues.

Some of the items the Aussie brought were identifiable, but not as to which person they may have belonged. There were belt buckles, pens, pieces of paper with a few words written, and forks and spoons from GI mess gear. He didn't bring out any larger pieces, although that may have been done later. One piece of paper that affected me the most was written on by a chap from Michigan. He had put down a date every day for ten or more days. The note was written quite clearly with a small comment about each day such as "Rainy," "God help us," "John died yesterday," "Plane overhead," and "Hopeless." Then the writing got very shaky. He skipped some days. When he returned to the diary, he was not sure how many days he had missed or what day it was. Then the diary stopped. Nothing.

On another sheet of paper the same lad had written that he wanted to open a restaurant in his hometown when he got back. He had planned a menu for each day of the week: Sunday: Chicken and dumplings; Monday: Hot beef sandwich with gravy; and so on.

Eventually, during the 1980s, a metal panel from the door of this plane was presented by the Air Museum in Port Moresby to the U.S. Air Force Museum at Wright-Patterson Air Force Base, Dayton, Ohio. The panel has names, initials, and other scratchings that are identifiable. The door panel may seem like a peculiar object to put in a museum, but there it is.

By now there had been quite a subtle transition in the way we were fighting the war. We no longer felt the desperation to get things done that we had felt up to this time. The navy was in control of thousands of square miles of ocean and had so many admirals they couldn't be kept track of. The infantry ground soldiers and the marines were on dozens of islands, not the two or three of a couple years ago. The air force had so many planes and they were bringing so many generals and colonels from the States that laundries had to be established so those officers could have clean shorts and shirts. In Troop Carrier, instead of two squadrons there were now so many squadrons that formed so many groups, they had to form a wing. A wing is a group of groups. Bomber and fighter plane units were growing so fast they had to form the Fifth Air Force. The Thirty-third was neither as important as it once was nor as critical to the war effort. However, we were one of the most decorated squadrons in the Pacific War. That distinction we earned.

Changes

A service-oriented newspaper was published down in Brisbane similar to the famous *Stars and Stripes* of the European theater. This newspaper was called *Guinea Gold*. It featured Stateside news, some international events, some political happenings, and a lot of coverage about which generals and which admirals were being promoted. There must have been some talk of eventually winning the war, and these high-ranking officers would need to have the publicity to become famous in order to keep their jobs after the war. I think the public information officer handling *Guinea Gold* was a one-star general.

Meanwhile, back in the United States, someone somewhere got the idea that the war bond sales effort would be helped if a beat-up old C-47 "Gooney Bird" were sent back to the States and flown around the country, with a real genuine combat crew making speeches and selling bonds. The crew must have been chosen by a Hollywood agent, because they took two good-looking sergeants as radio operator and crew chief. The pilots were Capt. Frank Libuse, operations officer of the Sixth Squadron, and our own Capt. Gene Glotzbach. They were sure a handsome foursome. They had clean shirts with pressed seams, trousers that fit, neckties (must have been shipped over special), polished Aussie fleece-lined boots, combat caps with no grease spots, and the biggest set of smiles loaded with straight white teeth ever seen in the Pacific.

That was a nice assignment, but I wasn't jealous about not being selected; maybe I came in second or third choice. When the select crew finished with that tour, they didn't even have to come back. After the luxury of the finest hotels and the classiest restaurants in the U.S.A., they wouldn't have fit in any longer with our company. They later claimed they raised enough money to finish out the war. Also, they admitted that they "had a pretty good time."

By now, Nadzab had become a giant air base. There was every type of aircraft there. I'm glad our seniority gave us the privilege of staying in Port Moresby. Our medical facility was still the small tent hospital, mostly filled with malaria patients and accident victims. But that wasn't good enough for giant Nadzab. What did they do? Someone called up the Mayo Clinic in Rochester, Minnesota, and asked them to send over some administrative people and to help build a big, new all-purpose hospital, fully staffed and equipped with all the latest machinery available. I was never in either hospital, but I heard theirs was a dandy—if you were sick, that is.

Among those fine fighter aircraft at Nadzab were several Black Widow, P-61 night fighters. They were the latest thing in modern tactical machines, equipped with expensive night-vision radar and vertical altimeter gauges. They were powered by two 2,000 horsepower Pratt & Whitney engines, giving them speeds even faster than the P-38s. The planes took off and landed at speeds greater than the pilots had been accustomed to in older aircraft. The Black Widows were also a lot heavier and more cumbersome than the sleek P-38s. The guys didn't like to fly them. There wasn't much call for night fighters yet, and since they had lost four Black Widows and their pilots in the first four weeks, there was almost a rebellion by the pilots. Instead of calling them Black Widows, the crews called them Widow-makers. No one had yet fired a shot at the enemy from these planes, which further made that attrition rate unacceptable.

Someone got the manufacturer to send out a test pilot to show how these machines should be used. That factory rep was Charles Lindbergh, a civilian. He gathered the Black Widow squadron around and told them coolly but authoritatively that it was a good airplane. He admitted it was a little hard to learn how to fly; however, it was powerful, fast, and an important part of the new air force arsenal. He then gave them ground lectures and a flight demonstration.

Lindbergh started out with a maximum performance takeoff run down the runway to normal lift-off position. Just as the gear came up, he shut off one engine. He climbed, gaining both altitude and speed on a single engine, made a medium-sharp turn, and circled back over the field at about 1,000 feet. As he approached the end of the runway, he pulled nose-up a bit and executed a smooth precision barrel roll while still on a single engine. He went on around, lowered the gear, taxied up to the pilots, and climbed out. A single-engine landing. Now I didn't witness this exhibition, but that's the way I heard it went. He went home. The pilots never bitched again about the Black Widow being a rotten airplane.

Now we were able to get our most experienced pilots rotated back to the States one at a time. Not because they were crazy, but because they had earned it. The rotation included radio operators and crew chiefs. New, rosy-cheeked kids came along to fill the vacancies. It was good to see them. They were fresh, eager, patriotic, and willing to learn a few tricks about how to stay alive from us old-timers. As an old-timer, I was twenty-nine years old.

Since we had an extra plane at least part of the time, we did some transporting of personnel down to the mainland for R & R. The two places were Rockhampton, not far from Townsville, and the big city of Sydney. These trips were primarily for the nonflying people. The flying crews saw new places all the time. Once when I was taking a load to Sydney on a night flight, someone came to the cockpit and said I had better come back to stop Jake from jumping out. Jake was a mature businessman from Great Falls. He owned the Club Cafe there and was in the military by his own choice. At one time, he was my adjutant. We were well acquainted and good friends. When I got to the back, I found Jake with a parachute strapped on, sitting against an emergency escape window. There must have been a bit of homemade juice brought along. (Note: We often had four parachutes on the plane, even though we might have twenty-five people aboard. And besides, I never heard of any C-47 crew bailing out and doubt that we carried chutes regularly.)

Jake had decided he would lean back against the escape window and when the time was right, he planned to pull the rip cord. He assumed that the chute would blossom out the window and carry him to earth. Since the window was about twelve inches by eighteen, it wasn't a very practical idea. If the chute did blossom, it would probably take only the part of the body in the harness along. This might leave Jake's head, arms, and lower legs behind. He didn't care. He had just always wanted to make a parachute jump.

169

There was much laughing and teasing, and I was not sure that he wouldn't pull that cord even if he couldn't get the window opened. A popped chute even inside the plane cabin could and would cause a lot of confusion. We got him away from the window and had more conservative guys sit there. Jake decided it wasn't such a good idea after all, and we got his chute off and stowed, under guard. I thought he was only fooling, but about half the guys didn't agree. I didn't see Jake many times afterward. He was soon promoted to group headquarters; he never did tell me if he would have followed through on his threat to jump. I'm not sure.

Sometimes on these R & R flights, the guys would carry a five-gallon jerry can of gas in their B-4 bag, with which they would buy the services of a cab driver while on leave. I imagine that practice was against regulations.

Some of them also learned, to their great relief, that when an Aussie lady said she was "all knocked up" she meant as all Aussies do, that she was tired.

Watson, who had flown over with the Thirty-third Squadron and was now CO of the Twenty-second, came over to visit his old mates and brought a pint of King's Crown. That was a homemade bourbon type drink aged about one month and available on the mainland from local bootleggers. The liquor was watered down about fifty percent, but that was acceptable. Watson was a true Texan in the sense that he enjoyed laughter and bourbon.

While he was visiting in our tent, we sipped some of his King's Crown. We always drank the sip to someone's health. We drank to the health of each of the three or four of us, to MacArthur, to Harry Truman, and to others. We had about run out of King's Crown at the same time we ran out of people whose health we wanted to acknowledge. Fortunately, Watson was able to spot our camp cleaner-upper, a fine black native gentleman whose name was Ichabad. Watson hollered out, "We drink to the health of Ichabad!" We all broke up laughing, probably the only time in New Guinea.

Now I know you don't think that is funny, but by golly, we did. Maybe it's because you didn't know Watson.

Shortly after this event, we had a pretty good-sized formation heading way up the coast almost to Wewak. I think it was forty or fifty troop carrier aircraft ferrying Aussie troops and supplies to a new battle zone. I was the flight leader. We picked up some P-38 fighters as cover as we passed Nadzab, but not many. Maybe eight or ten planes. With not enough for both close cover and high cover, the escort planes stayed down quite close to us and swept back and forth. We were flying across mountains, but well over them. We had to have the altitude above terrain in the event we had to turn and run. This was our privilege in case we were attacked. We would be a prize target for the Japanese with that many planes. And the Japanese had operational bases not too far away.

I spotted two aircraft at nine o'clock, about our altitude, and quite a distance away. I could just make out a silhouette, and they weren't P-38s. I asked the fighter flight leader if they were bogies. He said, "Yah, I see 'em. They are bogies to me." He sent over two P-38s to take a look. As the P-38s went toward them they just put on some speed, climbed, and left the 38s behind. A few minutes later the flight leader spotted them on the other side of us. Same thing. As the two 38s started to get close, the bogies put on the speed and disappeared. We didn't see them again. We completed our mission under tight cover by those concerned fighter pilots. They told us to expedite our unloading if we wanted them to go back with us. You can bet your "sweet patooty" (or whatever they said in those days) we wanted the cover.

An intelligence report confirmed a few days later that there had been two German Messerschmitt ME-109s doing something in our area. They must have been plenty good planes. Probably about like our P-51s, which were whipping both the 109 and 110 (twin-engine) German fighters over the English Channel. I'm glad the German's didn't have any spares to send to the Japanese.

Back on the base, squadron life went on as usual. For instance, Captain Bigger, our squadron engineering officer, had heard a rumor that there was an area in the extreme north of Australia where wild pigs could be found to hunt. New Guinea had no shortage of pigs, but the animals were held in such esteem by the natives, both as food and a sign of wealth, that none of the foreign visitors ever gave thought to killing a pig. As a matter of fact, pigs were so accepted within the society that native women on occasion suckled orphan piglets. Many Americans thought this a strange sight, but to the native this was a long established custom and considered most proper.

Bigger kept hounding me to take him to where the Cape York Peninsula pointed toward central New Guinea, so he could shoot a couple of pigs and bring them back to show off or give to the natives. His rumor had it that a certain local native there would take Yanks into the brush, where there was an abundance of pigs to hunt. After a while that seemed an interesting side trip to me. He got a crew chief to join us, and we three headed out for the small aborigine village of Yorktown, where there was a small airstrip. I think it was about 400 miles over water from Moresby and maybe 20 miles inland. No problem. We found the strip and started the search for the alleged guide.

Talking only pidgin English made the communication more than a wee bit difficult. After a while, we struck a deal with our guide. He started us back into the brush on a well-worn pathway. He jabbered constantly and kept saying, "pig," and pointing and changing directions, so we knew he must be an expert hunter. He carried a spear, but I don't know why. We walked for miles without even a single pig sign. We three wanted to head back, but our guide would have none of it. It was getting late and I was sure we would be lost, but obviously our guide didn't think so. He'd just point a different direction and jabber some more and say, "pig." We finally convinced him to head back, and of course all of us were disappointed.

172

Not too long after that, we saw a wild turkey in the brush. Bigger fired his .45 a time or two, but all he did was frighten the guide. I also carried my .45, but had the plane's trusty Tommy gun as well. Our guide suddenly gave us the sign to be quiet and hunker down, which we did. A few steps more and he pointed out not the pig we were expecting, but a turkey in a tree. As a true hunter, I knew you had to take your game when you saw it. I put the Tommy on auto and let go eight or ten rounds (seemed like a few hundred). Our guide picked up the bird, which appeared to be the size of a large chicken. There wasn't a whole lot left of the turkey. Maybe a single-shot .22 would have been a better weapon to use, rather than one that would lay down enough lead to bring down a small aircraft. I have a snapshot showing us with the remnants of the turkey being held high.

When we got back to the village, it was made plain to us that there were no pigs back there. The natives had hunted them almost to extinction. Maybe our friendly guide had actually got one some time before, or maybe we had been hoodwinked. I didn't care. I had my snapshot.

About this time, I had to take an Aussie official into Tsili-Tsili, for some reason I've long forgotten. Tsili-Tsili, which had been an important staging area for the large paradrop at Nadzab, had become a nonstrategic point. Therefore, military were no longer stationed there. The hubbub and activity during the preparations for the drop had really discombobulated the natives of the area. After all, they were so remote and isolated, they were most likely as primitive as any tribe in the country. They were considered by the Aussies to be one of the few tribes that had been headhunters in recent times. I didn't hear of them trying any of that white meat while our troops were there or since, but stories of their cannibalism of an earlier date were still told.

The area was totally without buildings or signs of white man habitation except the abandoned runways, and they were about half-overgrown with *kunai* grass. While waiting for the Aussie to

173

finish his business with his contact, my copilot and I went exploring back toward the grass huts of the few natives that lived nearby. The natives were not very friendly. Not unfriendly either, but timid and half-frightened. They were pygmies. We had heard about them but didn't accept the story for true until we saw them. They were about four and a half feet high, and their huts were about half as high as most other villages we had seen. For a long time after that I had a snapshot of the copilot standing beside a well-built round hut that had grass walls partway up and a doorway about as high as his belt line. Very few natives were visible, although a few were standing well back away from us and next to the bush. We didn't get a picture of any of them. They were probably glad to see us leave.

Another interesting flight mission occurred when a one-star general came around to organize both an itinerary and transportation for a USO group that would be in the area in a few days. Every entertainer or performer sent through by USO was excellent. Super. Good. And they worked their hearts out for no pay. They played an important part in the big "M" factor: morale. When I heard the credentials and the names of the entertainers, I knew right off they were no ordinary hoofers or song-and-dance-man group.

This group included Jack Benny, Carole Landis, Lanny Ross, Martha Tilton, and Larry Adler. Naturally, a well-known and talented group such as this should be given the very best attention available. A nice, clean airplane: no problem. A presentable crew chief and radio operator: no problem (we had lots of them). Copilot: we had a pilot named Monroe Adler, so obviously he should go along because of Larry Adler. Maybe they were cousins. But the pilot. Now that was a real problem. It should be someone who was intelligent, mannerly, capable, personable, and I suppose also thrifty, brave, clean, and reverent. I went through the list of our pilots several times but somehow just couldn't come up with the right name to assign to this unusual mission. There was only one solution: swallow your pride and be a good leader; take this job yourself. So I did.

174

They were a beautiful group. Very friendly, cooperative, pleasant, interested in everything, and interesting themselves. No fakes. Well, maybe Carole. She was Hollywood show business all the way. Tall, shapely, outgoing, vigorous, a real entertainer. She was married to an air force officer, Captain Wallace, who was stationed in the States. She was interested in airplanes and anxious to fly them. Or at least to help. She was invited forward to sit in the copilot seat while Monroe went back to visit Larry. A small idea emerged and we switched seats so she was in the pilot's seat. We had fighter escort. Not many. Maybe four or five P-47s, I think they were called Thunderbolts. They were big, fat, heavy fighters—not much good in a dogfight—so were probably available to go along as escort to a single Gooney Bird. I called the escort flight leader and asked him to send down a plane to look at my left engine area. Nothing serious, just needed someone outside to take a look. Reluctantly, he sent one down. The guy approached to about 100 feet out. He hated to slow down to our speed, but I kept saying, "Get in closer; get in closer." As he came in real close I told him to take a good look at the windshield area and the pilot's window to see if he saw anything unusual. He got in so close he could see inside the cockpit as well as I could. It finally registered on him that that blond, lipsticked, bare-shouldered, grinning, gorgeous apparition was a real live female woman. "EEEY-YOW!" was his loud, parting holler as he took off, doing rolls and barreling up to meet his buddies. I bet there was now no chance of a Japanese fighter plane getting anywhere near us.

Lanny Ross was a quiet, gentlemanly person with a perpetual smile. Sorta like the pictures of the good kid next door. For wholesomeness he could almost outdo Lawrence Welk.

Larry Adler was short, more businesslike than the others but pleasant enough. Not much of a visitor, but he could sure play that harmonica. He did it all the time.

"Liltin' " Martha Tilton was a doll. She was small, under 100 pounds. She was quiet and modest and pleasant, with a nice smile.

She was the vocalist with Woody Herman's band. An acquaintance of mine from college, Tex, was lead trumpet man in that band, so we had a mutual friend. She had a disadvantaged son (probably called retarded in those days) about whom she talked a lot. She worked to help him. I bet he was well cared for.

Jack Benny was plain worn out. He had been traveling and performing until he became ill. He was always pleasant enough, but quite subdued except when onstage. He was very interested in where he was and all the activities going on in New Guinea. He gave me his home telephone number in case I ever wanted tickets or whatever. I doubt if he expected me to come for dinner.

The USO representative (not the general—a civilian) was a paper busybody, which I suppose was his job. He did manage to get pictures and stories of this event into the Hollywood press and other newspapers. He also took many pictures of the local military with the entertainers and provided copies to the personnel. I have some that my mother collected, with me in them, of course.

Another popular entertainer who spent a long time in the area was Joe E. Brown. I never did see him or talk to him but understand he just stayed around in the area. He hitched rides anywhere and did impromptu bits or just ate with the guys and made them laugh. He had lost a son in this area; when or how I don't know. I guess he just felt like hanging around. Everyone liked him.

A goodly number of the old-time aircrews had either been returned to the States or been transferred into some of the higher levels of our Troop Carrier Command. That made me wonder just why was I hanging around. Should I go for a bigger job in group or wing? Perhaps if I did go for and get one of those positions, there might be another promotion or two. Then it would seem logical to apply to stay on in active duty status in the air force and go for a retirement. (Some of our flying and ground people did just that and retired after twenty or more years). While the promotion to group or wing would be much less hazardous work, it would be more responsibility. But who would want to make the military a career?

A visit from Colonel Adams, who was CO of group, gave us a chance to talk about just that. He'd been with General Kenney, and they bemoaned the lack of old-timers to bring into group and wing headquarters. All four of our original squadrons, the Sixth, Twenty-second, Twenty-first, and Thirty-third, had plenty of new bright, shiny guys, but they'd let just about all of our experienced personnel get away. Since I was in the latter classification, Adams asked, "What would you think if we made you a light colonel [lieutenant colonel] today, let you have thirty days Stateside, come back, we'll make you a bird [full colonel] in six months, but you never ask to go back again until we say so?"

I assumed that the proposition was from General Kenney. It would be a real sweet deal if one intended to make the military a career. Since I was eligible to rotate routinely, I had to make a decision pretty quick. My decision was handled real soon, probably by divine guidance. A navy officer came in and asked how he could get to Milne Bay, about 400 miles away. We hadn't been going to Milne Bay at all lately. I said, "I don't think we can help you now, but someone can within a few days. Besides, I can't worry about Milne Bay; I'm trying to figure out how to get to the States. I'm ready to go back."

"Hey, man, here's what I'll do. I'll trade you a ride on a luxury liner, with only about ten passengers aboard, from Milne Bay to San Francisco for a ride from here to Milne Bay."

And he could do it, too. The SS *Monterrey* had run aground on the north coast of New Guinea. They'd patched it up enough to more than likely get it back to San Francisco with just the crew and a few hitchhikers. No full load, too much risk?

"Buddy, you just made a deal," I replied. The boat would sail in three or four days. I had just time enough to get the paperwork under way, but to be sure, I had Mermelstein write up my own orders, got group's approval for what I was going to do, got them to get their paperwork out, flew the guy to Milne Bay late that afternoon, and finally got myself there with all my possessions in my B-4 bag with a day to spare. As the navy gentleman had promised, I had a first-class cabin all to myself, as did about ten other officers. We were the only guests aboard the ship.

Air transportation back to the States was hard to get, except for VIPs, and I wasn't one. So I decided an ocean cruise would be a good transition period. My mind was pretty well made up. I'd go into some kind of a business for myself at the end of hostilities and take my chances. Or maybe if I wanted an air force career, I'd have a chance at it later from Stateside.

I had never been aboard a cruise passenger liner before, and this one wasn't exactly like what paying passengers would experience during peacetime. Most of the ship had been converted and modified enough so it could handle about 7,000 troops, which was what it had been used for. Having only the ship's crew and about ten hitchhikers like myself aboard made it a high-class ride. We ate fine meals with the ship's officers. We had the run of the ship and played a thousand games of bridge. Officially, although we were all suffering from battle fatigue (sort of like running a couple of quarts low), we didn't think we were anything but normal. However, when a few of us convinced a medical doctor major that he should watch the water in his toilet each day to see which way it swirled when flushed in order that he could tell when he crossed the equator, there was probably some question about how normal we all were. Everyone knows that the seasons change between the northern hemisphere and the southern hemisphere when you cross the equator. The normal ocean current and the air movements are also opposite. Even the stars are different, like the Southern Cross and the North Star. But does the water in the toilet change direction? I don't recall.

We had no naval escort. Supposedly the authorities had determined the light-loaded *Monterrey* could outrun any Japanese submarine as long as the hole in the hull did not open up. I had no idea if we were going fast or slow. It was a beautiful ride, even with the occasional severe storms we plowed through. We never saw another ship or any plane during the sixteen days it took to reach San Francisco. Maybe the crew did, but they didn't talk to us about such things.

The scene was so peaceful aboard ship, it seemed like a proper time to reflect on what had happened during these past years. I thought about why life had been interrupted so violently and what had caused such a horrible mess. I wondered what would happen when the conflict ended, what it had done to us as individuals, and what would become of the U.S.A.

None of the answers were simple. There was a war in Europe in which we were involved as a friend and supporter of our allies. In the Pacific, someone had taken it upon themselves to take away land, places, and people that belonged to us. We don't take such an indiscretion lightly. Japan had one of the world's largest military machines with which to pursue their desire for more land to put their people on. Don't forget what they did! The Japanese bombed our fleet almost out of existence at Pearl Harbor. They were ruthless. They bombed and butchered the Philippines in brutal fashion. Remember the Bataan death march? The Japanese slaughtered 300,000 to 400,000 civilians in Nanking, China. Large numbers of Polynesians were eliminated. Aggression and expansion were what the Japanese had in mind, at the very least, for the entire Pacific, the Pacific Rim, Australia, New Guinea, the Solomons, New Zealand, and maybe even the United States.

I forgave and I do forgive, then and now. However, I cannot accept the underlying attitude they project, at Nagasaki for instance, when Americans visit their war memorial. Yet when they visit our memorial at Pearl Harbor (which they do daily, in numbers equal to our own U.S. visitors), their attitude is just that this piece of history should not have happened.

From a military standpoint, the Japanese were defeated when the United States regained possession of the Philippines. However, the Japanese maintained the barbaric concept of "kill Americans until we all die." I guess we don't think that way. Remember, it had

179

been established by military intelligence that we would lose between 1 million and 2 million U.S. personnel if we had to invade and subdue Japan proper. The Japanese were invited many times to agree to cease hostilities, but they would not. From a military perspective, I'm glad we dropped the atom bomb. However, I'm sorry that such a weapon does exist.

For me, leaving behind the dead and missing friends was quite traumatic, but I knew I could not belabor it then or now. There were so many. I was acquainted with only a few, but they all were very important to me and to their families. In retrospect, by the time I arrived at the combat area, I just accepted the fact that there was a real good chance that I would not return.

The Sigma Chi fraternity at the University of Montana lost more people during the war than any other fraternity in Montana and also more than any other Sigma Chi chapter in the whole United States. Montanans had certainly paid their dues the hard way.

Chapter 9
Back in the United States

On the SS *Monterrey*, it was a late afternoon day in the fall of 1944 when we first saw signs of San Francisco off in the distance. Seeing that Golden Gate Bridge from the other side was a thrill. The emotion on returning was just as great as the excitement felt when our little crew headed out away from it that night so long ago. During the rest of my life, each time I returned to the borders of the good old U.S. of A., whether by land, sea, or air, the thrill and the pride of being a citizen were still there.

While we were approaching and docking at Fort Mason, the ship's officers gave each of the passengers a few drops of spirits to toast our return. Which we gladly did. We were also informed that even though it was after working hours, someone in authority would be at dockside to welcome and receive us and process us. I didn't much care about that last word, but it turned out okay. I'm sure the officials didn't know who or what we were, nor why some passengers were reentering the States from a combat zone on a ship that was deadheading in for repairs. Anyway, they took us to an office by van and had some GIs handling our minimal baggage. They had us sit in nice easy chairs with drinks in our hands while they processed us. Processing took just a few minutes. As field-grade officers, we just had to sign a simple document saying we were who we said we were, that we were bringing no contraband into the United States, and specifying where we wanted to go for our reentry leave. When I said I wanted to go to Montana, I was told I'd best stay overnight and they would see I got a flight out to

Great Falls in the morning. One more night on a cot would not be the worst thing that could happen. As we started to each go our own way, the staff sergeant in charge asked me to wait a minute. He sorta whispered to me, "I have a single billet at the Mark Hopkins. Would you rather stay there or remain here at the fort?" I chose the Mark. The staff sergeant liked pilots best.

A military flight took me to Great Falls, where I was ushered into a building with a sign designating it *Headquarters Alaska Air Command.* I didn't like the sound of that "Alaska," but not to worry. A nice WAF sergeant volunteered to write some orders sending me to Santa Monica for reassignment, after some unknown number of "delay en route" days. She also gave me two gas ration coupons, each good for eight gallons of gas. I made some smart-aleck remark about having wasted a million gallons so didn't see why a few extra gallons now should be so critical. So she handed me two full books of coupons, enough to run a fleet of taxicabs for several weeks.

While in Great Falls, I borrowed a car from a friend and drove to Charlo. I got to Charlo in midafternoon on a Sunday. I drove toward the old house behind the store. There were cars parked everywhere. A bunch of people were standing in the yard, and there were good eats piled on a couple of card tables. Dad was on the sidewalk about halfway between the store and the house. He was standing his usual sideways, with his hat on. I went toward him. He gave me a quizzical look with this remark: "You must be George Junior. Haven't seen you around for some time. Have you been away?"

After my "delay en route," Santa Monica was a nice but short interlude. I was debriefed; why I don't know. I always presumed one of the debriefers was a psychologist who would determine my degree of "crazy"; however, one of the debriefers was the opposite. He wanted to make sure I could be polite and mannerly. I was no longer to say, "Pass the fuckin' butter." New clothes, new rules, new procedures, new U.S. Air Force—it all seemed very civilized. I even got a message to call a lady. She said, "My name is Maxine

Welden. My husband is Bob Welden from Lewistown, Montana. He is in England, and I am the governess for the Henry Fonda children. We occasionally enjoy having a Montana returnee join us for brunch. Would you please come out to the Fonda home on Tiger Tail Road about noon tomorrow?" Sure, why not? Especially now that I knew a few common words not to be used.

Bob Welden's father was the family doctor of almost everyone in Lewistown. Bob was currently a P-51 fighter pilot in England. Maxine had latched onto him while he was training in Arkansas, and she had somehow been hired to nanny the two Fonda children, Peter and Jane.

Mrs. Fonda was very gracious, as was Maxine. Henry was on duty elsewhere. They took me on a tour of the elegant home and showed me the pool. They even gave me a look at a whole drawer full of silk stockings. During WW II, Hollywood was patriotic, but not when it applied to silk hosiery. The maid/cook prepared a tasty repast, and Peter and Jane were asked to perform. They were probably about six and eight years old. They sang a couple of little ditties. One was a soft-shoe: "Tiptoe through the Tulips." Those kids were all right then. And, how's this for a coincidence: when we moved to Prescott, Arizona, two of the new neighbors in our subdivision were Bob and Maxine Welden.

When I returned to duty at Santa Monica doing nothing, I got a message from Colonel Imparato. He was CO of some kind of an outfit in Alabama and said he could use me. He also implied he could get me into the Command and General Staff School at Fort Leavenworth, Kansas. That is, if I had plans to stay in the air force. He was the guy that had bawled me out for coming on into Port Moresby on a single engine when my radio operator said we were about to ditch in the ocean. It was nice to be wanted, but I still didn't cotton too much to making the air force a career.

Pan American Airlines and Chennault's China Air Force also had application blanks for guys like me. But I took the advice of the guys at the officers' club and asked for assignment to the Big

Daddy of the troop carrier bases—Bergstrom Field, Texas. That I got, along with another week of "delay en route." I headed back for Montana.

Things around the old home had changed considerably. The store was still operating okay, and Joe and Margaret still owned their store and post office at the bison range at Moiese. Pink had been in the military at the Fort Monmouth Signal Corps facility in New Jersey. I guess Pink was by now, however, on his way to the Philippines with an advance cadre to set up a communications system in the Pacific theater. Fran was in the European theater with a hospital unit. Marney had matriculated at St. Catherine's College in St. Paul or was already a beautiful nun in the order of Sisters of St. Joseph. She must have been a good and intelligent Sister, because she became principal of numerous high schools in Minnesota thereafter. Gene either was in college at Mount St. Charles in Helena or had already gone to the Wharton School of Finance at the University of Pennsylvania. Jim and Ski were married, but I can't remember just when, even though I asked them six months ago and they told me. Obviously, I'm unable to get my relative time frames in order. Remembering is a fleeting talent!

Bergstrom Field was a major air force base facility. It still is to this day. The base's total population when I got there was about 15,000 military and 5,000 civilians. Bergstrom's principal mission at that time was the training of troop carrier flight crews, in both C-47 and C-46 aircraft. A number of our Thirty-third crew chiefs and radio operators were at the base, as were two of my old pilot pals: Glotzbach and Franni Schnieders. The base commander was Col. Sam Davis from the North African theater. He was unaffectionately known as "Sergeant" Sam because of an unfortunate incident in which he was involved over Sicily. The story was that he had been the flight leader of a group of troop carrier aircraft loaded with paratroopers heading for Italy, or thereabouts, when several of the planes were shot down by guns on U.S. Navy vessels. Colonel Davis was busted to sergeant and sent home for his part in the fiasco. However, when he got home to face court-martial it was determined that he was leading his formation exactly on course. He was aware that the flight would pass over a U.S. Navy flotilla, but the navy had failed to inform some of its gunboats about the friendly overflight. Thus the navy was responsible for the tragedy. Sam got his Eagle back and was given the big job as CO of Bergstrom.

During my reentry briefing at Bergstrom, I had learned there was a proper military protocol for reporting in to a new assignment; on the assigned day the base adjutant took me through the proper door to say hello to Sam. Even his own adjutant had to rap on the door—one knuckle, one rap—before entering. I did my imitation of a brisk walk to within two steps of Sam's desk, uncovered (cap under left arm), gave a brisk salute, and made this very proper announcement: "Sir, Major Wamsley, reporting for duty, as ordered."

Sam gave me a quick return salute, stood, and shook hands. "George, good to see you. Sit down. I want to hear about New Guinea."

So we had a good lengthy exchange of views and opinions and drank a few cups of coffee. I guess we got along just fine.

My assigned duty was to be CO of Squadron G, which meant nothing to me, yet. The adjutant took me over to the "G" area of the base to give me a brief orientation prior to my first day on the job, which would be tomorrow.

This was a squadron much different than any I had previously known. We were not to be involved in any flight training, no operations, no maintenance, no ground school. In fact, not much. It appeared to me I was a sort of house mother for six or eight hundred officers who were at this base to participate in flight training. Some were brand-new second lieutenants just fresh from aviation cadet schools. Some were ground officers of every rank out of air force units around the world. Some were from the other military services. The one thing they did have in common was a desire to become a rated pilot before the war went out of business so that they could have a specialty in the aviation industry.

The adjutant explained that once a month about 300 officers would be sent out without fanfare, assigned to an air-active troop carrier outfit or back to their previous military organization with a new secondary qualification as pilot. Three hundred new ones would show up and go through the same rigamarole once a month, so there was always a bunch of new faces. Our management team was "yours truly," a second lieutenant, and a staff sergeant. Squadron G counted in its inventory five or six two-story barracks, conventional army style, that were known as visiting BOQs, where most of the temporary guests lived. The visiting officers had their own mess hall. (We base personnel had our own facilities, which included a nice club about one block from my office location.) The quartermaster took care of all the needs of these people. Operations took care of their flight training. Someone took care of their ground school, and they got paid regularly by someone. I couldn't figure out just what my burden might be.

The adjutant said, "I suppose I might as well tell you what the bad news is right now. We have a 'Pass-in-Review' one Saturday a month at 0900 hours, promptly, on the main taxiway in front of the tower. All military units are required to participate, if not otherwise occupied, and since there is no scheduled flying training on Saturday mornings, your squadron, G, will be there in proper dress, in their entirety. All of them. You can form up here on the parade ground in front of the barracks and march them over to the taxiway. I'll show you the best streets to take to get there.

"We have about fifteen separate sections, and that is a mighty big bunch of people. The band arrives early and will be in position, facing the reviewing stand, at the south end of the taxiway. Your section is next to the band, and you are to march your people into position about forty feet to the band's left and halt in a straight line and dress up [meaning lineup] with their front line. Since G is a large group you use a sixteen-man front."

My immediate thought was, *My Gawd! How do you turn corners with sixteen guys in each line bumping into each other?* Each of those sixteen columns would be fifty or sixty men long. That would be almost the size of the Soviet infantry marching past Stalin at their May Day parade.

The adjutant took me to my new office and introduced me to the outgoing CO, who appeared to be very happy to be leaving; the second lieutenant, who was a true Alabama southerner, a good guy; and the staff sergeant, who was owner of a small business in Detroit, too old for the draft, but doing his duty and doing it very well. Our office was located in a single-story building and had paneled walls and nice furniture. I couldn't understand how come it was upgraded from the usual GI standard until I saw the rest of the building. A door leading out through our office opened on a carpeted hallway, which ran to the other end of the building just like a hotel hallway. And that's what it was. There were four deluxe rooms on each side with private bath, carpeted floors, and all the amenities that we had forgotten about while overseas. Just outside were two tennis courts and the path to the officers' club, which was about half a block away. These rooms were reserved for visiting dignitaries or other VIPs. It gave me, the lieutenant, and the sergeant a sense of power to think we got to pass on just who was worthy to be billeted in our Waldorf Astoria accommodations. Unless, of course, the base commander asked us to put someone up. Then we said, "Yes, sir."

All of the above gobbledegook is getting around to a time where I can tell you about my first Pass-in-Review, which was coming up day after tomorrow at 0900 hours. I've always wondered if I could live through telling about it. But I guess I made it through back then so should not hyperventilate over just writing down some of the highlights here and now.

The first order of business of my first day on the job was a council of war with the lieutenant and the sergeant. The problem was easy to define: "How in hell do we get these guys into a formation and down to the parade position and then make them look

187

like a military unit instead of a herd of people as we pass by the reviewing officers?" We had a large inventory of officers, almost 1,000, the sergeant said, but 2 of them were full colonels: one was infantry and one was an air force ground officer. "Great idea, we'll have one of them do the honors. They sure outrank me," I suggested. Both said absolutely not, or something similar.

My partners explained the procedures previously used by my predecessors. The day began with reveille at 0430 hours. I jumped out of my skin. My next question was: "What do we do until nine o'clock?"

The response was: "Well, the men dress in the uniform of the day and then form-up on the parade ground in front of our barracks at 0600 hours, then two hours taking roll call and getting into a ragtag formation. We are lucky to get in review position by 0900 hours, because everyone is pissed off and beginning to look raunchy because we've been sweating a couple of hours by now."

A number of our members lived in town (Austin), and they sure hated the hurry-up-and-wait routine, so I'd say the attitude of the men was very poor. We finally decided I would put an informal notice on our bulletin board. The notice went something like this:

TO: EVERYONE

We are scheduled to Pass-in-Review Saturday at 0900 hours, in front of dignitaries in the reviewing stand near the tower. They expect all of Squadron G to participate.

Since my only marching experience was from our barracks to the mess hall at Kelly Field a long time ago, I realize I don't know enough marching commands to use up the usual time allotted. We will dispense with reveille, roll call, and the preliminary form-up.

We will ALL be ready to move out at 0800 hours in a sixteen-man front, pointed in the right direction.

Be prompt. Be ready to move out. Don't argue with me when I give an improper command. We all know where we are headed.

With your total cooperation we will be ready to Pass-in-Review before 0900 hours.

If this new schedule works out satisfactorily it will be S.O.P. hereafter.

Signed: ME

They loved it. On Saturday morning at 0750 hours I was out in front of eight or nine hundred officers lined up sixteen abreast and about fifty or sixty deep. The lieutenant was two steps ahead of the man on the extreme right of the first line. When I hollered, "Dress right" (after having hollered, "Ten-shun," of course), every man jack of them turned his head right, put his right arm out from his side, and touched the shoulder of the man on his right, ending up with the approximate proper spacing between individuals. After a few minutes of shuffling, the lusty command of "eyyyes—front" brought us to the end of step one. We were at attention and ready to move out. By the grace of God we didn't miss 0800 hours by more than a smidgen.

There were about four ninety-degree turns getting out to the end of the taxi strip, but all our guys knew what we wanted to do and where we wanted to go. Therefore, as we came to each intersection along the route, regardless of what kind of a command I gave, they did the right thing. Turning a formation that large at a street corner that was quite narrow had a real jam-up potential. It was like a wagon wheel with the hub being stationary, but marking time while the spokes of the wheel adjust the size of their steps out to the rim, where those guys are at the end of "pop the whip" and darn near running. We made a big loop out in the wide open spaces so we could approach the band, plus about forty feet, from the rear. We got the front of our group halted right in line with the front of the band while those farther behind jockeyed back and forth until they were about where they should be. I turned to face my men and gave them a big "dress right—hup," and they lined up and spaced up just like a bunch of marines would do.

My lieutenant was his two steps ahead of the right front man of the formation. Usually he would be in the center, but I had a reason this time. Just behind him was one of the bird colonels, and behind the colonel was some other officer. Those three had a potential part to play that my staff and I had discussed.

After an "eyyyes—front" and a "paraaade rest" (feet slightly spread and hands clasped behind your back), I had to do an "about-face" and so had my back to the troops and my eyes toward the reviewing stand.

Now, add that it was a hot and muggy morning to the pressure of getting this maneuver accomplished today, and there was some question in my mind if I'd stay upright or keel over somewhere along the parade. There were about six or eight medical ambulances stationed behind our twelve or fifteen different sections. Someone else must have thought there was a good chance for a number of the less stalwart to faint or keel over. If I did such an embarrassing thing, those three officers on the right-hand corner were to take care of removing and replacing me. Ugh! I didn't want to do that. Incidentally, the medics took care of a number of casualties that day, but thankfully, I was not one of them. I sweated a lot and quivered some and worried a little.

After an eternity (probably fifteen minutes) standing at parade rest while all sections got into position, someone in authority hollered, "Pass-in-Review!" In true military fashion there was a lot of transferring of the identical message from one big shot to someone almost as big and he in turn to someone a little less important. This occurred two or three times until finally no one else answered. That must have been the signal for some high-ranker way over by the reviewing stand to call out, "Commandant of troops, reeeport!"

The commandant then had to do an about-face and yell at the unit commanders, "Reeeport!" He had different sections beginning with the band about a quarter of a mile to his left, on down to the Military Police, which was about a quarter of a mile to his right. He had to be able to yell real loud. I've forgotten the unit name for the band, but their leader came back to the commandant with a loud, brisk, clipped abbreviation of, "All present and accounted for, sir." This came out very clipped, about like this: "All prez' 'count' for, sir." The commandant saluted him, which meant he could unsalute briskly. Then it was my turn. I gave him an identification loud enough to be heard in Dallas: "Squadron G, all prez' 'count' for, sir!" He touched his hat and I snapped my arm to my side and stood at attention along with my troops, until the reporting had been completed down through the MPs.

I was sure there were some members of old Squadron G who weren't present or accounted for, but I was certain the commandant didn't want to visit about the absentees in my outfit or any of the other units. Everyone was reported accounted for, although by now some were resting at or near the ambulances.

When the "all present and accounted for" had been completed, the commandant of troops did an about-face and told his superior (perhaps that was the base commander) what had been accomplished. The base commander must have been well pleased, so far, and his guests sitting in the shaded reviewing stand must all have been in attendance, because he told the commandant to "Pass-in-Review." The commandant did another about-face, and facing his troops, he really let go a long, loud, and drawn out: "Paasss-in-reeeviewww."

Obviously that was the signal for the band to break into one of John Philip Sousa's best. They did a "column right, for'd march," and they were off and heading away from the reviewing stand. In about fifty yards they took a "column left" and shortly thereafter another "column left," and then they were heading down toward the reviewing stand, exactly as they should have been.

I got my guys tucked in behind the band, and where the band went we went. As we approached the reviewing stand, I had to turn around and march backward (without tripping), facing my troops to give a confident "squadronnn—eyyyes right." This they did (and

I think they saluted also) in order that they get to see the VIPs for whom this show was put on. Another half-mile or so down the taxiway we pulled to a halt and the troops were dismissed to find their own way back to the barracks or wherever they chose to go. Most had the balance of the day off.

It was a good, disciplined show. I later saw photos of this day's event, and they really looked good. The troops stood tall. The lines were straight, and all marched in unison. The base CO said he was pleased. Things didn't go too badly! But I was sure glad the marching was over. I went by the office, got a cold shower to soap off the sweat, put on a clean uniform, and headed to the officers' club for lunch. The adjutant was there. He said, "Hey, you looked great! Calm, cool, and confident. I'll buy you a drink!"

The Squadron G guys were so pleased with the new timetable for the parade that they all promised to show up on time next time. I recall only one or two more of these performances during my time at Bergstrom, but they were no sweat. A piece of cake.

Apparently Sergeant Sam or some of his subordinates decided I didn't have enough to do. Periodically I'd receive orders appointing me to miscellaneous, but very important, boards. Those appointments included the Venereal Disease Control Board, the Tire and Gasoline Rationing Board, the Court-martial Board General, the Court-martial Board Special, and, best of all, the Officers' Club Board of Directors. I liked that last one because the club had a lot of money and I helped hire some big bands for Saturday night parties.

It was understood that I would participate in some flying missions, and sure enough, one came along before I'd really gotten into the swing of how the base functioned. For some reason long forgotten, several C-47 loads of people had to be delivered to Chanute Field, just outside of Chicago. Maybe six or eight planes, and I was to be the flight leader, probably because I was green card instrument-rated. The flight shouldn't have been any big deal, except that there was some rather severe thunderstorm activity about halfway between Bergstrom and Chanute. The trip was not planned as a formation flight, just all planes in the same general area.

We had lots of interplane chatter until we reached the frontal line of that thunderstorm. The weather began to get kind of rough, and there was a lot of lightning straight ahead. The weather reports for farther ahead were all okay, but no one reporting seemed to know how thick or how severe the frontal line was. The front was too long to try to go around either end. I faced a dilemma.

My preference was to go to an alternate field and wait out the storm, which by now I knew was real bad. Later I might then find that the other planes had gone on through. If they were at Chanute wondering where the hot-shot green-card, experienced leader was and why he had lost his nerve because of some bad air and lightning they would think I was a sissy. On the other hand, my goose would really be in the fire. By then, the static was so bad we had no communication between planes. My pride was at stake. I plunged on through. The trip was a bad ride for quite a few miles. After getting out the other side of the storm, I could only raise two planes, but we continued on to Chanute. It was a worrisome time on the ground at Chanute until we finally located the other planes. They were piloted by guys with enough common sense to turn around and seek safe shelter on the ground until conditions improved. The planes were scattered over several states, but all had landed safely.

Knowing that those planes were safe was a relief, but I knew I had made a serious mistake. Our three pilots that went through the storm didn't do any bragging about having done it. The trip back to Bergstrom was uneventful. That was real relief.

One day during the usual busy time, the control tower received a message: "Bergstrom Tower, this is Lt. Jay Ottman. I'll be landing in fifteen minutes. I'll be seeing Major Wamsley. Please send out a car. What runway shall I use?"

The tower guys blinked a bit. Unannounced visitors seldom dropped in. But the tower did answer, "Use 180 South. Call in on your base leg. What is the rank of the highest officer on board?" After all, Lieutenant Ottman might have General Old aboard.

Jay came back with, "Second lieutenant."

With that the tower called and asked if I was expecting a Lieutenant Ottman. I said, "I wasn't expecting him, but I'd like to see him. Will you let him land?"

"Roger, will do."

The tower got him into the traffic pattern, landed, and had him park his single-seat fighter plane right in front of Operations. They sent out a car with a driver and delivered him over to Squadron G. It gave the flight line a little break in their busy routine. Jay's explanation to me was that he was on a cross-country from his base and just decided to stop by for a social call.

About this time, I recall another incident at Bergstrom. Colonel Nigro of Operations called and asked if I'd like to fly copilot on a C-46 from Bergstrom to Spokane the next day. I'd never even been in a Curtis C-46. They were twice the size of the C-47s and handled twice as much cargo, but the C-46 was a two-engine airplane. Because the cruising speed was almost twice that of the C-47, I was anxious to fly in one before I separated from the military.

On this flight we had the usual crew chief and radio operator, plus about twenty-five middle-aged, intelligent-talking, reserved men, dressed in new military khaki uniforms without any insignia or identification visible. Our destination was Spokane, but the passengers were to go to Hanford, Washington. They turned out to be scientists working on something called atomic energy. They were very poor flying passengers. By the time we had been airborne an hour or two, at least one passenger decided to give up his breakfast. The crew chief was able to provide him with a "honey bucket." The ensuing unpleasant odor and bumpy air made the rest of the passengers queasy beyond control, to the point that there were no more containers to pass around. When you are airsick and you gotta go, you go.

I guess the scene was a helluva mess. Our crew chief suggested we, the crew, exit by a front escape door when we landed at Lowry Field, Denver. We were glad we did. As the passengers came down the steps, they were white, green, and sick. Most of them just hit the ground prone, wishing they were dead. Nigro offered to buy them lunch, but I don't think he had any takers. The crew chief got a detail of maintenance men, and they soon had the plane in good shape, except for the Lysol odor, by the time we were ready to head for Spokane. All of our victims were reluctant but got aboard.

As we passed over the Continental Divide between Butte and Helena (I suppose we were up about 12,000 feet), I asked the colonel if I could do a little buzz job on my home village of Charlo. It was practically on our path. We turned off the autopilot, and I started pushing the nose down. As we approached the Mission Range, a couple of things became evident. We were approaching the buzz zone a lot faster than I expected, and also there was still about 3,000 or 4,000 feet of altitude to burn off. When I first saw Charlo it seemed a lot closer to the Mission Range than I remembered from my Cub airplane days, when buzzing was about 95 mph, and now at about 300 mph it was approaching very fast. I got the plane down to about 300 feet altitude just as we reached the city limits. I don't know how fast we were traveling. The wingspread reached almost all the way across town, and I bet the "whoosh" we made was pretty scary to the cats and dogs and cows. Nigro made a figure-eight turn to give old Charlo a second helping while I wrote on a piece of cardboard: *Sorry, can't stop now. G.W.* and pushed it out the window. The wind tore it into four pieces, three of which were found and taken to my folks. The next time I saw the Charlo farm people, several of them thanked me for flying over their place. They thought I'd singled out their places, and they appreciated it. Actually, with that big machine, going that fast, just to pass directly over Charlo twice took a turn from Crow Creek to Post Creek and back again.

We delivered our load of scientists safely in Spokane. They played a part in the successful mission by *Enola Gay*, which dropped the bomb on Hiroshima not long thereafter. And you might recall that bomb got the Japanese folks' attention.

Shortly after I returned to Bergstrom, a minor skirmish occurred at Squadron G. My sergeant asked me to come with him into the barracks next door. He didn't say why. We went through the back door into the lower-level latrine area. There, right over a row of fixtures, at eyeball height, was a poster about eighteen inches by twenty-four on a bright red background. Centered was a good photo of a handsome black gentleman, just his face and shoulders. Above the photo in large black print was the word WANTED. The photo was of our good and loyal orderly, who had faithfully and efficiently kept this barracks in tip-top condition. The officers made their own beds. He did the rest. The name of the orderly was in medium-sized print just under the photo. Then along the bottom in small print were these words: "Anyone other than the above individual seen loitering on these premises is to be reported to the Military Police at once." I asked the sergeant if any of the other barracks had similar pictures like this. "Yes, sir. Every barracks has pictures of their orderlies, both downstairs and upstairs." I said, "I guess I'd better make a call."

The CO of the MPs was a captain. He was a tough, small person from Georgia and probably a good policeman. He was also on the VD board, so I did know him.

"Captain, what gives with these new posters in the latrines in our barracks over here?" I asked.

"Oh, they are just to scare off any unwelcome visitors."

"Well, I don't like them."

To which he responded, "If you'd take the trouble to read the whole thing you'd see it wasn't a 'wanted poster' for your man."

In my best "I'm your boss" voice, I said to him, "If you will take the trouble to come over here and get those things down, in the next few minutes, all of them, I'd sure appreciate it. I have one of

196

them in my office, but the rest are to be destroyed." I didn't know if I had that authority or not, but they were removed, posthaste, and the subject wasn't brought up again.

One time as CO of the group I did have a little problem with one of our guest officers. The problem was 1st Lt. Edward P. Something. Someone must have considered him a good officer somewhere, or else he'd never have been promoted to first lieutenant.

Edward would go to Austin on Saturday night and get about half-drunk. Maybe it was more than half. He would become unruly enough that the city police would pick him up. They would turn him over to the MPs, who in turn would bring him to his barracks and send him to bed. I guess this had happened more than once, but the time it happened on my watch was more serious. On this occasion Edward wanted to act crazy after he got in his room, so he took his .45 and started shooting at the stovepipe, which went up through the ceiling. The guys sleeping on the upper floor didn't care for that at all. The base MPs got there in a hurry and took his gun away. Next morning there was a report of the incident from the MPs saying that disposal of the case was up to me. I had no idea what to do, but I had Edward P. Something come in for a visit. He was fine, didn't seem to think it was a big deal, and left with, "Have a good day." Sort of old buddy like.

When I called the adjutant to tell him I had a little problem and was wondering if I should take it up with the base CO he laughed and said, "Edward P. ———? He is always in trouble." I wondered aloud why someone hadn't tried to straighten him out, but the adjutant said it had been tried. He also told me that Edward P. had some relative in a very high place, which was why no discipline had been recommended in the past. I asked if there was any chance he might be transferred. The adjutant came back with, "If you don't want to do any disciplining of this guy I might just be able to ship him out to a place that is a bit less civilized."

"That would be just fine with me," I said. I never saw Edward P. again, but I did buy the adjutant a drink. Okay, I took the easy way out.

Shortly before the end of the war with Japan, when victory was assured, the workload around Squadron G was not heavy. My tennis game was improved. I didn't get to fly much. Well, one occasion to fly would have been interesting, so here goes: Colonel Nigro asked if I'd like to do a glider snatch with him. Heck, yes. I'd heard it was being done, but I'd never seen it done and had never talked to anyone who had done one. The snatch involves hanging a hook out the back of the plane, while in flight, to catch a tow cord that is suspended on two poles thirty feet in the air and attached to a glider. When the hook catches the cord, the cord begins to tighten up, the hook snaps firmly closed, and the cord plays out the rear of the plane, gradually increasing tension until the line is taut. And eventually the glider moves and increases speed and becomes airborne. All well and good.

During the war troop carriers had been towing gliders a lot of places. I never did. The main difference between towing and a snatch is that in the snatch the towing plane is not on the ground with the glider. In towing both planes are on the ground; a line runs from the tail of the tow plane to the nose of the glider. The tow plane performs a normal takeoff, and the glider follows. Both get airborne.

During this flight the plane, with Colonel Nigro as pilot, had just hooked the cord attached to the glider when something went wrong. All of a sudden the slack in the cord was taken up between the planes. The airplane jolted, and the glider moved forward about ten feet. The line broke, and Nigro said, "Ah, shit!" He was very disappointed. There were a lot of people watching the demonstration. The mechanical failure didn't bother me, though. I was just a last-minute pickup copilot, and no one pays any attention to who he is. That was my first and last experience as a tow pilot.

198

My final duty formation was just for Squadron G, no Pass-in-Review. My request for separation had been approved, and orders sending me to Hill Air Force Base, Utah, were delivered to my desk Friday afternoon, effective Saturday. There was no way to call off the formation, so the squadron lined up, expecting to put up with miscellaneous routine activities for an hour or so. When I went out in front of them the lieutenant had them at attention and I gave them parade rest. I told the lieutenant, "No formation. No inspection. No assignments." I waved a copy of my orders, shook hands with the lieutenant, and told him to turn 'em loose. On this day, they could do whatever they wanted to do. I walked away. Some of them cheered. Not many and not for long, but I swear I heard some cheers!

It was a wonderful feeling to be in the United States. God bless America.